English Touring Theatre and York Theatre Royal
present the world première of

BRIDESHEAD REVISITED

the novel by Evelyn Waugh
adapted by Bryony Lavery

GW00455770

First performed at York Theatre Royal
on 22 April 2016

Cast (in alphabetical order)

Anthony Blanche / Father Mackay / Samgrass	Nick Blakeley
Charles Ryder	Brian Ferguson
Lady Marchmain / Nanny	Caroline Harker
Julia	Rosie Hilal
Cara / Celia	Samantha Lawson
Cordelia	Kiran Sonia Sawar
Lord Marchmain / Mr Ryder	Paul Shelley
Sebastian	Christopher Simpson
Bridey / Kurt / Rex	Shuna Snow

Creative team

Writer	Bryony Lavery
Director	Damian Cruden
Designer	Sara Perks
Lighting Designer	Richard G. Jones
Sound Designer	Yvonne Gilbert
Composer	Chris Madin
Casting Director	Polly Jerrold
Associate Director	Kirsty Patrick Ward
Movement Director	Philippa Vafadari

Production team

Production Manager	Felix Davies
Company Stage Manager (York)	Anna Belderbos
Company Stage Manager (tour)	Mark Shayle
Deputy Stage Manager	Robyn Clogg
Assistant Stage Manager	Rosanna May Simpson
Assistant Stage Manager*	Judith Volk
Wardrobe Supervisor (York)	Hazel Jupp
Wardrobe Mistress (tour)	Charlie Baptist
Relighter	Zanna Woodgate
Set Construction	Harrogate Theatre Scenic Services / AWAV Workshops
Production Sound Engineer (tour)	Simon McCorry
Rehearsal Photographer	Helen Maybanks
Production Photographer	Mark Douet
Press Representation	Kate Morley PR
Marketing Consultants	Joe Public

Special thanks to:
Evelyn Waugh Estate, Leslie Woolford, Joyce Meader, Castle Howard Estate, Stephen Joseph Theatre, DAW Logistics and Copperfield Studios

Welsh College of Music and Drama Placement.

Cast

NICK BLAKELEY
Anthony Blanche / Father
Mackay / Samgrass

Nick trained at the Bristol Old Vic
Theatre School and Bristol
University.

Theatre credits include: *A Woman
Killed with Kindness*, *13*, *Damned
By Despair* (National Theatre); *The
Sunshine Boys* (Savoy Theatre);
Hapgood (Hampstead Theatre);
I Heart Catherine Pistachio (Soho
Theatre); *The Last of the De Mullins*
(Jermyn St Theatre); *Happy Never
After* (Pleasance); *Hard Feelings*
(Finborough Theatre); *24 Hour
Plays* (Old Vic), *Millennium*
(Vineyard Theatre, New York, Old
Vic New Voices).

Television credits includes: *The Old
Bailey*, *Doctors* (BBC).

BRIAN FERGUSON
Charles Ryder

Theatre credits include: *The Broken
Heart*, *The Changeling* (The Globe);
Hamlet (Citizens Theatre); *Adler &
Gibb* (Royal Court); *Threeway*
(Invisible Dot for Edinburgh
Festival); *The Game Show*, (Bush
Theatre); *The Aztec Trilogy*.
Richard III, *Dunsinane* (Royal
Shakespeare Company); *Money*
(The Arches); *Earthquakes In
London* (National Theatre);
Shakespeare in a Suitcase (Royal
Shakespeare Company); *The Dark
Things*, *Fall* (Edinburgh Traverse);
The Drawer Boy (Glasgow Tron);
Black Watch, *Rupture* (National
Theatre of Scotland); *Snuff*
(Glasgow Arches/National Theatre
of Scotland), (*Poorboy*).

Television credits include: *Line of
Duty*, *Our World War*, *Field of
Blood: The Dead Hour*, *Doctors*,
One Minute Drama: The Prayer,
River City, *Taggart: Island*,

Film credits include: *Imagine That
King*, *Voices*, *The Woods*, *Residue*.

CAROLINE HARKER
Lady Marchmain / Nanny

Caroline trained at the Central School of Speech and Drama.

Theatre credits include: *The Railway Children* (York Theatre Royal at Kings Cross Theatre); *Blithe Spirit* (York Theatre Royal); *Pride and Prejudice* (Open Air Theatre, Regent's Park); *The Village Bike* (Sheffield Crucible); *The Railway Children* (York Theatre Royal @ Waterloo Station); *Tusk Tusk*, *The Strip*, *The Editing Process* (Royal Court); *All Mouth* (Menier Chocolate Factory); *Entertaining Angels* (Chichester Festival Theatre and tour); *Present Laughter* (No. 1 Tour); *Battle Royal* (National Theatre); *Falling* (Hampstead Theatre); *Things We Do for Love* (Duchess Theatre); *Life Goes On* (Basingstoke Theatre); *A Mongrel's Heart* (Royal Lyceum); *Hidden Laughter* (Michael Codron Ltd/West End) and *Sweet Charity*, *Daisy Pulls it Off*, *Don Juan* (Harrogate Theatre).

Television credits include: *Doctors*, *Coronation Street*, *Holby City*, *New Tricks*, *The Commander*, *Head Cases*, *Margaret*, *Murder In Suburbia*, *Foyle's War*, *Auf Wiedersehn Pet*, *Hans Christian Andersen*, *I Saw You*, *Armadillo*, *Keeping Mum*, *A Touch of Frost*, *Kavanagh QC*, *Casualty*, *A Dance to the Music Of Time*, *Holding On*, *Moll Flanders*, *Harry Enfield and Chums*, *Honey for Tea*, *Middlemarch*, *Covington Cross*, *Riders*, *Growing Rich*, *Casualty*, *Chancer*.

Film credits include: *Lady Godiva: Back in the Saddle*, *A Woman of The North*, *The Madness of King George*.

Radio credits include: *If I Should Go Away*, *Westwood*, *Mrs. Henderson's Xmas Party*, *Best Foot Forward*, *The Golden Pavements*, *The Swish of the Curtain*, *Still Life*, *Barcelona Bird*.

ROSIE HILAL
Julia

Theatre credits include: *The Oresteia*, *Measure for Measure*, *Antony and Cleopatra*, *Holy Warriors* (Shakespeare's Globe); *The Hard Problem* (National Theatre); *The Hypochondriac* (Shakespeare's Globe, The Wannamaker Theatre); *All's Well That Ends Well*, *As You Like It*, *Hamlet* (Royal Shakespeare Company), *Occupied* (Theatre 503).

Film credits include: *London Road*.

SAMANTHA LAWSON
Cara / Celia

Samantha trained at Bristol Old Vic Theatre School.

Theatre credits include: *Julius Caesar* (Royal Shakespeare Company/ BAM/Moscow Arts Theatre); *Peer Gynt* (*Nationalteatret*, Norway); *The Changeling* (ETT/Nottingham Playhouse); *His Dark Materials* (National Theatre); *The White Witch and Flesh to a Tiger* (Talawa Theatre Company); *King John* (The Union Theatre/Steam Industry); *Oedipus Rex*, *Antigone*, *Young Oedipus* (The Scoop); Red Noses (Bristol Old Vic Theatre); *Asylum Dialogues* (Tricycle Theatre); *Rendition Monologues* (Amnesty International/Actors for Human Rights); *Great As I Am* (Nordic Black Theatre, Norway); *A Tribute to the Heroes* (Operahuset, Norway); *One Language Many Voices* (TNT Theatre/ADG, Germany); *The Maids* (Workhorse Productions); *Voices from the Edge* (Union Chapel); *Still* (Cockpit Theatre); *Fantasy* (C+Edinburgh/Greenwich Playhouse); *Abolition of Slavery* (British & Natural History Museums, Yaa Asantawaa); *The Asylum Monologues* (Ice and Fire Theatre)

Television credits include: *Occupied* (Cahtrupart, Yellow Bird/TV2, Norway),*Toast* BBC.

Film credits include: *Generation Mars* (*NRK/DNF*); *Julius Caesar* (BBC/Illuminations/RSC); *Poverty* (Ice and Fire), *The Dark Is Rising* (Fox/Walden), *Random Acts* (Random Acts), *Understanding Slavery* (Harvest Films), *Hong Kong* (Norwegian Film Institute), *Ladies* (Bristol Old Vic), *Cross Knowledge* (Mas Productions France); *Abolition of Slavery* (British/Natural History/ Imperial and Bristol Museums)

KIRAN SONIA SAWAR
Cordelia

Kiran trained at the Oxford School of Drama.

Theatre credits inclde: *Cyrano De Bergerac* (Southwark Playhouse); *Aladdin* (Oxford Playhouse); *The Caucasian Chalk Circle* (Unicorn Theatre); *My Name Is . . .* (Arcola Theatre/UK tour); *Unspeakable Crimes* (Ice & Fire/Actors for Human Rights); *2050: The Future We Want* (United Nations, Geneva), *Defining Moments of Truth and Deception* (Soho Theatre).

TV/Film credits include: *Legends*, *Holby City*, *Murdered by My Father*.

Film credits include: *Forced Marriages* (dir. Ruth Beni), *Pardes* (dir. Myriam Raja).

PAUL SHELLEY
Lord Marchmain / Mr Ryder

Paul trained at RADA.

Theatre credits include: *All My Sons* (tour); *Long Day's Journey into Night* (Lyceum, Edinburgh); *The House That Will Not Stand* (The Tricycle); *Macbeth*, *King Lear*, *The School for Scheming* (Orange Tree Theatre); *King Lear* (Royal Theatre, Bath); *Medea* (No. 1 Tour); *Earthquakes in London* (No. 1 Tour); *Moonlight*, *The Family Reunion* (Donmar Warehouse); *A Voyage Round My Father* (Salisbury Playhouse); *Macbeth* (Chichester, West End, New York); *The Merchant of Venice*, *Absurd Person Singular*, *The Invention of Love*, *A Man for All Seasons* (West End); *The Secret Rapture*, *The Crucible*, *Hedda Gabler*, *Lady in The Dark* (National Theatre); *Les Liaisons Dangereuses*, *The Winter's Tale*, *The Twin Rivals*, *Dingo*, *Bingo* (Royal Shakespeare Company); *Julius Caesar*, *Antony and Cleopatra* (Shakespeare's Globe).

Theatre Directing credits include: *The Seagull* (Orange Tree Theatre); *A Man for All Seasons* (York Theatre Royal).

Television includes: *Paradise Postponed*, *Titmus Regained*, *A Tale of Two Cities*, *Morse*, *Secret Army*, *Midsomer Murders*, *Heartbeat*, *Revelations*, *Dr Who*, *Blake's 7*.

Film includes: *Oh! What a Lovely War*, Polanski's *Macbeth*, Rupert Goold's *Macbeth*, *Caught in the Act*, *It Shouldn't Happen to a Vet*.

Audio book credits include: *The French Lieutenant's Woman*, *The Kingsley Amis Trilogy* and many Robert Goddard thrillers.

CHRISTOPHER SIMPSON
Sebastian

Theatre credits include: *Forests*, directed by Award-Winning Catalan director Calixto Bieito (international tour); *Leaner Faster Stronger*, directed by Andrew Loretto (Cultural Olympiad at Sheffield Theatres); *The Knowledge*, directed by Charlotte Gwinner, *Little Platoons*, directed by Nathan Curry (Bush Theatre); *Fallujah* directed by Jonathan Holmes (Truman's Brewery); *The Bacchae of Baghdad* directed by Conall Morrison (Abbey Theatre), *Pericles* directed by Adrian Jackson (Royal Shakespeare Company/Cardboard Citizens); *Fragile Land*, directed by Paul Miller (Hampstead Theatre); *The Ramayana*, directed by Indhu Rubasingham (National Theatre); *Double Tongue*, directed by Michael Walling (Old Red Lion), *Off the Wall*, directed by David Glass (David Glass Ensemble).

Television credits include:
Shameless, *All about George*, *State of Play*, *Second Generation*, *White Teeth*.

Film credits includes include:
Sixteen, *The Day of the Flowers*, *It's a Wonderful Afterlife*, *Brick Lane*, *Mischief Night*, *Chromophobia*, *Code 46*.

SHUNA SNOW
Bridey / Kurt / Rex

Theatre credits include: *Twelfth Night* (The Rose, Bankside); *Aftershakes* (Marlowe Theatre, Canterbury); *Palindrome* (Arcola); *Little Stitches* (Bare Truth Theatre Co/Theatre 503/Arcola/The Gate); *Iron* (Bold Over/Old Red Lion); *Hamlet* (Actors from the London Stage/US tour); *Top Girls* (Mercury Theatre Company, Colchester); *Engaging Shaw* (Vienna's English Theatre); *The Charity That Began at Home* (Orange Tree Theatre); *Comus* (London Handel Festival); *Welcome To Ramallah* (Iceandfire/ Arcola Theatre/York Theatre Royal); *Tongues* (Menagerie Theatre Company); *Going Potty* (Ranjit Bolt after Georges Feydeau, Menagerie Theatre Company); *Julius Caesar*, *Death of a Salesman*, *Iph*/Colin Teevan after Euripides, *Iphigeneia at Aulis*, *The Winter's Tale* (Mercury Theatre); *Me And*

the King (Manchester Royal Exchange Studio); *Poor Mrs Pepys* (New Vic, Stoke); *Separate Tables* (Manchester Royal Exchange); *Absurd Person Singular* (Oldham Coliseum); *Betrayal*, *Resistible Rise of Arturo Ui*, *Ion*, *Road*, *The Triumph of Love*, *All My Sons*, *Oh! What a Lovely War*, *The Three Sisters*, *Romeo and Juliet*, *The Caucasian Chalk Circle*, *Uncle Vanya* (Mercury Theatre Colchester); *Macbeth* (Westcliff Palace Theatre); *A Shoemaker, a Gentleman* (Shakespeare's Globe); *Cymbeline*, *Kenneth's First Play*, *Little Eyolf*, *Much Ado About Nothing* (Royal Shakespeare Company).

Television credits include: *The Royal Today*, *Midsomer Murders*.

Radio credits include: *Baldi*, *With Great Pleasure at Christmas*, *The Pallisers*, *Les Misérables*, *Voices from Vindolanda*, *The Charterhouse of Parma*, *Nicholas Nickleby*, *The Life of the Bee*.

Film Credits: *Orna* (BAFTA, short film screening).

Creative team

BRYONY LAVERY
Writer

For ETT: *Thursday* (ETT/Brink, Australia).

Other plays include: *A Wedding Story*, *Last Easter*, *Her Aching Heart* (Pink Paper Play of The Year 1992), *Smoke*, *Dirt*, *More Light*.

Her play, *Frozen*, commissioned by Birmingham Repertory Theatre, won the TMA Best Play Award, the Eileen Anderson Central Television Award and was then produced on Broadway where it was nominated for four Tony Awards. *Stockholm*, for Frantic Assembly won the Wolff-Whiting award for Best Play of 2008. *Beautiful Burnout* for The National Theatre of Scotland and Frantic Assembly received a Fringe First at Edinburgh, before productions in the UK, New York, Australia and New Zealand.

Stage adaptations include: *101 Dalmatians* (a musical for Chichester Festival Theatre 2014); *A Christmas Carol* (Birmingham Rep/Chichester Festival Theatre); *Precious Bane*, *The Wicked Lady*, *Treasure Island* (National Theatre 2014-15) and *Behind the Scenes at the Museum* (York Theatre Royal).

Recent work includes: *The Believers* (Frantic Assembly); *Queen Coal* (Sheffield Crucible), *Treasure Island* (National Theatre). She is currently writing *Slime* (for Banff Centre, Canada), *The Parting Glass* (for Manchester Royal Exchange), *The Lovely Bones* (for Birmingham Rep) and developing *Dying Light* for TV.

She is a member of the Royal Society of Literature, an honorary doctor of Arts at De Montford University and an associate artist of Birmingham Repertory Theatre.

DAMIAN CRUDEN
Director

Damian has been Artistic Director of York Theatre Royal for the past 19 years. He trained at the Royal Scottish Academy of Music and Drama between 1982 and 1986.

He has directed many productions, including: *In Fog and Falling Snow*, *The Restoration of Nell Gwyn*, *Blithe Spirit*, *The Legend of King Arthur*, *The Guinea Pig Club*, *The York Mystery Plays 2012*, *Laurel and Hardy*, *Forty Years On*, *Peter Pan*, *My Family and Other Animals*, *The Railway Children*, *To Kill a Mockingbird*, *The Wind in the Willows*, *Up the Duff*, *The Homecoming*, *The White Crow* (Eichmann in Jerusalem); *Death of a Salesman*, *Patient No. 1*, *Enjoy*, *Bouncers 2007 Remix*, *The Dumb Waiter*, *The Hare and the Tortoise* (also Japan), *Pygmalion*, *Broken Glass*, *East Is East*, *Hay Fever*, *Macbeth*, *A Cloud in Trousers*, *Brassed Off*, *Caitlin*, *A Taste of Honey*, *Habeas Corpus*, *Up'n'Under*, *Frankenstein*, *Noises Off*, *Little Shop of Horrors*, *Othello*, *Closer*, *The Turn of the Screw*, *Bedevilled*, *A Funny Thing Happened on the Way to the Forum*, *Behind the Scenes at the Museum*, *Kafka's Dick*, *Man of the Moment*, *Having a Ball*, *Romeo and Juliet*, *Getting On*, *The Three Musketeers*, *Les Liaisons Dangereuses*, *All My Sons*, *Piaf*, *Dead Funny*, *Educating Rita*, *Frankie and Johnny in the Clair de Lune*, *Neville's Island*, *Multiplex*, *Abandonment*, *Private Lives*. He has co-directed the last 19 York Theatre Royal pantomimes with Berwick Kaler.

Before York, Damian worked for various regional theatres as a freelance director. He was Associate Director for Hull Truck in the early 1990s and prior to that Co-artistic Director of the Liverpool Everyman

Youth Theatre. He worked for the Tron and TAG in Scotland and was a tutor for the Scottish Youth Theatre.

SARA PERKS
Designer

Sara holds an Edinburgh Fringe First; the John Elvery Theatre Design Award and a Vision Design (Costume) Award from the BBC. She has recently been nominated for both Broadway World Awards (Set Design and Costume Design) and a What's on Stage Award (Set Design) for *American Idiot*.

As Associate Designer with English Touring, credits include: *The York Realist* (UK tour and West End); *King Lear* (Old Vic), *Romeo and Juliet* (National tour and Hong Kong Arts Festival). Other credits for ETT include: *Eden End*.

As Associate Artist at Mercury Theatre, Colchester, credits include: *Saturday Night and Sunday Morning*, *Quadrophenia*, Pink Floyd's *The Wall*, *Depot*, *Journey's End*.

Current projects include: Green Day's *American Idiot* (National Tour), *Private Lives* (Mercury Theatre, Colchester).

Theatre credits include: *Any Means Necessary* (Nottingham Playhouse); *Footloose* (UK tour); costume design for *The Snow Queen* (Royal & Derngate); *Blood* (Tamasha); the first UK production of *Dancehall* (CAST); *How to Breathe* (Nottingham Playhouse); *Betty Blue Eyes*, (Mercury/West Yorkshire Playhouse/Liverpool Theatres/Salisbury Playhouse),*The Glee Club* (CAST, Doncaster); *Hello Dolly!*, *Gypsy*, *Hot Stuff!* (Curve, Leicester), *The King and I* (Curve/national tour); Tennessee Williams' *Spring Storm* in rep with Eugene O'Neill's *Beyond the Horizon* (National

Theatre/Royal & Derngate); *Wind in the Willows*, *Alice in Wonderland*, *The Wizard of Oz* (Royal & Derngate); Neil La Bute's *Helter Skelter/Land of The Dead/The Furies* (touring for The Bush and Dialogue); *Forgotten Things*, *Ugly* (Red Ladder); *The Ring Cycle Plays* (Scoop, London); *Treasure Island* (Derby Playhouse); *The Elixir of Love* (Grange Park Opera, co-design); *Return to the Forbidden Planet* (national tour); *Dead Funny* (Oldham/national tour); *The Crypt Project* (site specific at St Andrews Church, London, for Sincera); *The Ladykillers* (Exeter Northcott); *Union Street* (Plymouth Theatre Royal's millennium project).

She also designed the original and several subsequent productions of the cult space-rock musical *Saucy Jack and the Space Vixens*.

RICHARD G. JONES
Lighting Designer

Richard lit the Broadway production of *Sweeney Todd* at the Eugene O'Neill Theater, for which he won a Drama Desk Award for Outstanding Lighting Design. He was nominated for a TMA Theatre Award for Best Lighting Design for *The Railway Children* at the National Railway Museum as well as a DORA award for the Toronto production.

Current projects: *Sister Act* (UK Tour, Leicester Curve and Jamie Wilson Productions); *Celebrating Christmas with the Salvation Army* (Royal Albert Hall).

Theatre credits include: *Behud* (Soho Theatre); *City of Angels* (Bridewell Theatre); *Bouncers* (Whitehall Theatre); *Journey's End* (Octagon Theatre Bolton); *Other Desert Cities*, *Good People*, *The Collector*, *Venus in Fur*, *Breaking the*

Code, Good People ((English Theatre Frankfurt); *Noises Off, The Hired Man* (Octagon Theatre Bolton); *The Railway Children* (York Theatre Royal, Kings Cross Theatre); *The York Mystery Plays* (York Museum Gardens); *All Quiet on the Western Front* (Nottingham Playhouse); *The Guinea Pig Club, All My Sons* (York Theatre Royal); *Whiter Than Snow* (Graeae); *Amy's View, The Rubenstein Kiss* (Nottingham Playhouse); *Twelfth Night* (Bolton Octagon Theatre/York Theatre Royal); *Chicken Soup with Barley* (Nottingham Playhouse); *My Family and Other Animals* (York Theatre Royal); *Death of a Salesman, A Taste of Honey, Wind in the Willows* (York Theatre Royal) abd *Peter Pan* (Oxford Playhouse).

UK national tours include: *Fiddler on the Roof* (Music and Lyrics); *Calamity Jane* (Jamie Wilson Productions); *Beautiful Thing, Wuthering Heights* (OTTC); *Rasputin* (Natural Theatre Company); *Candide* (Ivy Arts Centre Guildford); *The Hot Mikado* (for Watermill Theatre); *Canterbury Tales* (Northern Broadsides); *Spongebob Squarepants the Sponge that Could Fly* (Broadway Asia); *Accidental Death of an Anarchist* (Northern Broadsides); *To Kill a Mockingbird, The Diary of Anne Frank* (Touring Consortium); *Strictly Come Dancing* Arena Tours (Phil McIntyre Productions/Stage Entertainments/BBC Worldwide); *Harry Enfield and Paul Whitehouse Legends Tour*.

West End credits includes: *Sunset Boulevard, Sweeney Todd, The Gondoliers, Mack and Mabel, Carmen, When Pigs Fly, Steptoe and Son, Horrid Henry Live and Horrid*.

CHRIS MADIN
Composer

Chris has written original scores for more than 150 productions for theatre, film, television, dance and radio. He composed this score for the Olivier Award-winning stage version of *The Railway Children* in 2008 and he received a Dora Award nomination for the music when the show transferred to Toronto in 2011. Chris was also Artist in Residence at University College Bretton Hall for three years. He has held music workshops at The Globe and for the National Youth Theatre. His corporate work has toured throughout Europe and Australia.

Theatre credits for York Theatre Royal include: *The Wind in the Willows, The 2012 Mystery Plays, The Guinea Pig Club, Laurel and Hardy, Peter Pan, Two Planks and a Passion, My Family and Other Animals, The Crucible, To Kill a Mockingbird, Coram Boy, Twelfth Night, Death of a Salesman, A Man for All Seasons, Rabbit and Hedgehog, Pinocchio, Bouncers, Broken Glass, Pygmalion, Hobson's Choice, Macbeth, The Beauty Queen of Leenane, Brassed Off, The Pocket Dream, A Taste Of Honey, Caitlin, Private Lives, Abandonment, All My Sons, A Midsummer Night's Dream, Othello, The Blue Room, The Three Musketeers, Behind the Scenes at the Museum, The Chrysalids, Habeas Corpus, Up 'n' Under, The Glass Menagerie, Frankenstein, The Snow Queen, Having a Ball, Disco Pigs, Romeo and Juliet*.

Other theatre credits include: *Steptoe and Son In Murder at Oil Drum Lane* (Comedy Theatre, West End); *The Crucible* (Bolton Octagon); *A Cloud in Trousers* (Southwark Playhouse); *Ay Carmela* (Shaw Theatre); *The Lifeblood* (Edinburgh Festival/Riverside Studios); *Romeo* and Juliet (Tidelines), *Frog and Toad*, *The Snow Queen* (Crucible Theatre, Sheffield); *Passion Killers*, *Up 'n' Under 2*, *Bouncers*, *Laurel and Hardy* (Hull Truck Theatre); *Beauty and the Beast* (Chester Gateway), *Misery* (King's Head).

Television credits include: *Two Lives*, *One Body; The Escape Artist*.

Radio credits include: *Behind the Scenes at the Museum*, *The Midnight House*, *The Lifeblood*, *The Midwich Cuckoos* (nominated for the Sony International Radio Drama Awards).

Commercial credits include: *More Th>n* insurance, *Maryland Gooeys* (*VCCP*), *Fisherman's Friend* (Fallon), *Timepilot* (Star).

YVONNE GILBERT
Sound Designer

Yvonne spent many years as a Musical Theatre Operator in the West End before working as a Sound Manager at the National Theatre.

Theatre credits include: *Voysey Inheritance*, *King James Bible*, *Statement of Regret* (National Theatre); *Twelfth Night* (Regents Park); *The Eighth Wonder of the World* (Brunel Museum); *American Idiot*, *Legally Blonde*, *Man of La Mancha* (Bridewell); *On the Town*, *Lift*, *Ghost*, *Addams Family*, *Rent*, *Twang*, *Touched*, (Guildford School of Acting); *Singer* (Bernie Grants Arts Center); *Jacques Brel is Alive and Well* (Mountview); *Breed* (Theatre 503).

Sound Associate credits include: *Only the Brave* (Millenium Center); *84 Charring Cross Road* (Salisbury Playhouse); *Rapture, Blister, Burn* (Hampstead); *Finding Neverland* (Leicester Curve); *Privates on Parade* (Noël Coward); *A Chorus Line* (Palladium Theatre); *Peter and*

Alice (Noël Coward); *August Osage County*, *Time and the Conways*, *Phaedra*, *Danton's Death*, *Greenland*, *Juno and the Paycock* (National Theatre).

POLLY JERROLD
Casting Director

Prior to becoming a freelance casting director Polly worked as Casting Associate at the Royal Exchange Theatre on a wide range of productions from the world premiere of Simon Stephens' *Punk Rock* to a co-production of Bernstein's *Wonderful Town* with the Hallé Orchestra under Sir Mark Elder.

Polly continues to enjoy a close relationship with the Royal Exchange in a freelance capacity along with casting numerous productions for the Birmingham Repertory Theatre.

Recent Birmingham REP credits include: *Of Mice and Men*, *Anita and Me*, *A Christmas Carol*, Rachel De-lahay's *Circles*, Steve Thompson's *Feed the Beast* and a large-scale tour of *The Government Inspector* as part of the collaborative *Ramps on the Moon* initiative.

Other recent credits include: *Beyond the Fence*, a new musical for Sky Arts, Wingspan and Neil Laidlaw Productions; Margaret Edson's *Wit* (Royal Exchange); Arnold Ridley's *The Ghost Train* (Royal Exchange/ Told by an Idiot); *Peter Pan* (Regent's Park); *James and the Giant Peach* (West Yorkshire Playhouse); *Rumpelstiltskin* (the egg at Theatre Royal Bath); Ella Hickson's *Merlin* (Royal & Derngate/ Nuffield Theatre) and *Little Shop of Horrors* (Royal Exchange).

Polly is currently casting a feature film based on Catherine Bruton's novel *We Can Be Heroes* as well as *Educating Rita* (Hull Truck), *The*

Hound of the Baskervilles (York Theatre Royal), *Peter and the Starcatcher* (Paul Taylor-Mills and Royal & Derngate) and a major new production of *Wonderland* (Neil Eckersley Productions, directed by Lotte Wakeham), the recent Broadway musical hit which will tour the UK in 2017.

KIRSTY PATRICK WARD
Associate Director

Kirsty is Artistic Director of Waifs + Strays theatre company and has just completed the National Theatre Studio Director's course. She was shortlisted for the JP Morgan Emerging Directors award in 2013 and was selected as a 2012 finalist for the JMK Young Directors Award. She is currently a director for National Theatre Connections and also took part in the Old Vic New Voices TS Eliot US/UK Exchange in 2011.

Director: *Chef* (Soho Theatre 2015/ Fringe First winner, Edinburgh Festival, 2014); *NFTS Screenwriters Graduation Showcase* (National Film & Television School/ Soho Theatre); *I'm Not That Kind of Guy*, *Mary Louise* (The Vaults); *Evita* (MT4Youth/Belfast); *Comets* (Winner Ideastap Summer Brief 2014/Latitude/Festival No 6); *People Like Us* (Pleasance); *Snow White* (Old Vic/Educational Tour); *Chavs* (Lyric Hammersmith); *Present Tense* (Live Theatre); *Brave New Worlds* (Soho); *Life Support* (York Theatre Royal), *New Voices 24 Hour Plays 2011* (Old Vic).

Associate Director: *Communicating Doors* (Menier Chocolate Factory);

Theatre Uncut flagship tour 2014 (Soho/Regional Tour), *Symphony* (Watch This Space/NT/Latitude Festival), *Young Pretender* (Edinburgh/regional tour).

Assistant Director: *Arcadia* (English Touring Theatre); *King Lear*, *Othello* (Shakespeare's Globe); *Our New Girl* (Bush Theatre); *Bunny* (Fringe First winner, Edinburgh/ regional tour); *The Boy on the Swing* (Arcola).

PHILIPPA VAFADARI
Movement Director

Philippa is movement director for a number of theatre companies including Boilerhouse Theatre, Vamp Productions and Communicado. She formed BandBazi (Circus Theatre Company) in 2001, which specialises in fusing aerial circus with theatre. For BandBazi, her work as choreographer and performer includes *Pussy Galore's Flying Circus* (UK and Germany), *Suzy=Soraya*, *Nearly Mine*, *The Persian Cinderella* (UK tour), *Love Indeed* (UK tour) and *Mind Walking* (UK and Indian tour). Philippa played Audrey Hepburn and Holly in BandBazi's *Breakfast at Audrey's* which won an Edinburgh Fringe First for new writing in 2005. She is currently in development for *Hamlet Asylum Seeker* in association with Talawa Theatre Co. In 2016/17 she will be researching a new piece of theatre in Iran collaborating with Don Quixote theatre company, funded by the British Council. Philippa previously choreographed for York Theatre Royal's production of *King Arthur* (2013).

ETT
ENGLISH
TOURING
THEATRE

English Touring Theatre is one of the UK's most successful and exciting production companies. At the heart of everything the company does is the passionately held belief that people throughout the country expect and deserve theatre of the very highest quality imagination and ambition.

THE HERBAL BED
Spring 2016

THE ODYSSEY: MISSING
PRESUMED DEAD
Autumn 2015

A MAD WORLD
MY MASTERS
Spring 2015

ETT IN NUMBERS

23 Years
1.6 Million Audience Members
735,710 Minutes of Theatre
1,631 Creatives, Designers and Performers

> **"English Touring Theatre is surely the national theatre of touring."**
>
> Sir Ian McKellen, patron

ABOUT US

Patrons Sir Ian McKellen and Stephen Mangan
Director Rachel Tackley

Executive Producer	**Production Manager**	**Administrator**	**Finance Officer**
Jane Claire	Felix Davies	Annabel Winder	Di Penty
Producer	**Production Assistants**	**Intern**	**Marketing Consultant**
James Quaife	Bridie Donaghy	Chloe Brass	Joe Public
Associate Producer	Floriana Dezou	**Head of Finance**	**Press Representation**
Jeremy Woodhouse		Stephen Penty	Kate Morley PR

Supported using public funding by
ARTS COUNCIL ENGLAND

ett.org.uk

York Theatre Royal has been producing bold and original drama since 1744 and welcomes 200,000 people each year. In 2015 and 2016 the theatre closed for a £6 million redevelopment, the largest investment in the building in 50 years. It opened in April 2016, welcoming its audiences back with the world premiere of *Brideshead Revisited*.

We've been a core part of our city for 270 years, and we've become even closer to our community by staging large-scale volunteer productions. In 2012, 1,700 members of our community put on the *York Mystery Plays*, and in 2015 we followed suit with *In Fog and Falling Snow*, in which community actors and behind-the-scenes staff joined forces to dramatize the rise and fall of York's Railway King George Hudson. The number of young people involved with York Theatre Royal has also risen dramatically: our youth theatre is one of the largest in the country, with 16 groups and almost 400 members.

YORK MYSTERY PLAYS 2012

THE RAILWAY CHILDREN

The theatre has found huge success from its own productions, most recently with *The Railway Children*, which premiered in York in 2008 and was awarded the Olivier Award for Best Entertainment. Last year this family show was restaged in York and London, and in March 2016 a stage-to-screen adaptation of the York production aired in over 400 UK cinemas. Our much-loved pantomime also draws visitors from all corners of the globe. The country's longest-running dame, Berwick Kaler – about to celebrate his 38th year in a York panto – and regular cast members Martin Barrass, Suzy Cooper and David Leonard, have a devoted regular audience.

Collaborative work is at the heart of York Theatre Royal's output: *Lord of the Flies* and *Blood + Chocolate* (with Pilot Theatre; the latter also with Slung Low); and *Princess and the Pea* and *Rapunzel* (with tutti frutti) are some of the acclaimed co-productions we've had a part in. It has been a privilege to work with English Touring Theatre on this production of *Brideshead Revisited*, and we look forward to a long partnership with its brilliant team.

DICK WHITTINGTON (AND HIS MEERKAT)

BOX OFFICE: 01904 623568   yorktheatreroyal.co.uk   Registered Charity no. 229396

CITY OF YORK COUNCIL

Supported using public funding by

ARTS COUNCIL ENGLAND

LOTTERY FUNDED

Brideshead Revisited

Bryony Lavery's plays include *Frozen* (TMA Best Play, Eileen Anderson Central Television Award and four Tony nominations), *Stockholm* (Wolff-Whiting Award, Best Play, 2008), *Beautiful Burnout* (Fringe First), *A Wedding Story*, *Last Easter*, *Her Aching Heart* (Pink Paper Play of the Year, 1992), *Dirt*, *The Believers* and *Queen Coal*. Her stage adaptations include *101 Dalmations*, *A Christmas Carol*, *Precious Bane*, *The Wicked Lady* and *Treasure Island* (National Theatre). She is a member of the Royal Society of Literature, an honorary Doctor of Arts at De Montford University and an associate artist of Birmingham Repertory Theatre.

Evelyn Waugh (1902–1966), English writer, regarded by many as the most brilliant satirical novelist of his day. Son of the publisher Arthur Waugh, he was educated at Lancing College, Sussex, and at Hertford College, Oxford. His first great success as a writer was *Decline and Fall* (1928), followed by *Vile Bodies* (1930). Subsequent novels include *A Handful of Dust* (1934), *Brideshead Revisited* (1945) and *The Loved One* (1948). Waugh became a Catholic in 1930. He travelled extensively throughout the 1930s and wrote several travel books. His Second World War trilogy, published collectively as *Sword of Honour*, comprised *Men at Arms* (1952), *Officers and Gentlemen* (1955) and *Unconditional Surrender* (1961).

Brideshead Revisited

a play by
BRYONY LAVERY

adapted from the novel by
EVELYN WAUGH

FABER & FABER

First published in 2016
by Faber and Faber Limited
74–77 Great Russell Street
London WC1B 3DA

Typeset by Country Setting, Kingsdown, Kent CT14 8ES
Printed in the UK by CPI Group (UK) Ltd, Croydon CR0 4YY

Based on the novel *Brideshead Revisited* © Evelyn Waugh, 1945

This adaptation © Bryony Lavery
and the Beneficiaries of the Evelyn Waugh Settlement, 2016

A CIP record for this book is available from the British Library

ISBN 978-0-571-33293-9

2 4 6 8 10 9 7 5 3 1

Brideshead Revisited in this adaptation was presented by English Touring Theatre in a national tour which opened at York Theatre Royal on 23 April 2016. The cast, in alphabetical order, was as follows:

Anthony Blanche / Father Mackay / Samgrass /
  Nick Blakeley
Charles Ryder Brian Ferguson
Lady Marchmain / Nanny Caroline Harker
Julia Rosie Hilal
Cara / Celia Samantha Lawson
Cordelia Kiran Sonia Sawar
Lord Marchmain / Mr Ryder Paul Shelley
Sebastian Christopher Simpson
Bridey / Kurt / Rex Shuna Snow

Director Damian Cruden
Designer Sara Perks
Lighting Designer Richard Jones
Sound Designer Yvonne Gilbert
Composer Chris Madin
Casting Director Polly Jerrold
Associate Director Kirsty Patrick Ward
Movement Director Philippa Vafadari

Characters

Charles Ryder
Hooper
Sebastian
Anthony Blanche
Nanny Hawkins
Mr Ryder
Hayter
Julia
Rex Mottram
Cordelia
Bridey
Lord Marchmain
Lady Marchmain
Cara
Samgrass
Kurt
Celia
Father Mackay
Wilcox
Plender
Footman
Doctor

Each member of the company plays both English society
in all its many glories . . . and their specific parts

How It Works

*'My theme is memory, that winged host
that soared about me one grey morning of wartime.'*

We are in the Second World War.

There are the barest minimum of useful artefacts.

Because mostly it is where memory arrives
in a succession of images . . .

Each location we visit has its particular tones
and colours in Ryder's, and our, mind . . .

All performers are, until required, sort of assistants –
like the Wakikata of Noh theatre – who become
what we need for the memory evoked.

All scenes and characters should appear surprisingly
like memories do.

Everything is sort of late-at-nightish, until it flares
into colour and line when a memory arrives . . .

There is music.

There are the faintest suggestions of houses, countries.

There are drinks.

Servers of drinks.

Various listeners . . .

It is all incredibly artful
and theatrical and beautiful.

BRIDESHEAD REVISITED

for Damian Cruden
co-creator

The odd line lengths
weird   spacing
and plethora of exclamation marks
and question marks in the text
are the author's attempt to convey
the frenetic nature of these characters
in their situation!!

In the text / indicates one character
talking over another

Act One

ONE

Total darkness . . . until . . .

Ryder
> . . . the blackout
> just after love had died between me and the army . . .
> We arrived somewhere by train in the dead of night,
> just before dawn . . .
> My adjutant said . . .

> (*Hooper appears.*)

Hooper
> The house is up here
> This way, sir.

> (*Exterior footsteps.*)

> Frightful great fountain.
> All rocks and carved animals.
> Come in.

> (*Vast door opens.*)

> Great barracks of a place
> I've just had a snoop round.
> Very ornate.

> (*Interior footsteps.*)

> Look in here . . .!!

> Queer thing, sir, it's a sort of private personal Roman
> Catholic church
> You never saw such a thing.

Ryder
And I said
Yes, Hooper, I did.
I've been here before.

Hooper
Oh well, you know all about it.

Ryder
Yes I know all about it.
This place is Brideshead.
I came here
With Sebastian
my first year at Oxford . . .

(*Hooper disappears.*)

TWO

Ryder experiences a mixed arrival of Brideshead memories.

Sebastian
Oh Charles, don't be such a tourist!

Cara
He is dying of a long word.

Lord Marchmain
And you . . .
You will no doubt
Become an official war artist . . .?

Nanny
Ring the bell.
We'll have tea.

Sebastian
Shall we try a bottle from every bin?

Lord Marchmain
The Chinese Drawing Room.
And Wilcox . . .
The Queen's Bed.

Lady Marchmain
We must make a Catholic out of Charles . . .

Cordelia
Rex's tortoise has disappeared.

Samgrass
You find me in solitary possession of this magnificent house!

Bridey
Julia . . .
Where are Mummy's jewels?

Cordelia
Send Sebastian my special love.

Julia
Your poor face . . .

Cordelia
I think perhaps he is afraid of the dark . . .

Julia
Papa . . . it's Bridey's . . .

Cordelia
I've just seen Sebastian . . . he's awfully drunk!

Lord Marchmain
I think I shall give it to Julia and Charles . . .

THREE

Tom bell tolls curfew . . .

Ryder

My room is heavy with
Smoke
My mind quite weary with metaphy / sics

Voices

Hold up! He's swaying! He's leaning!
Come *on? Get hold of him! Hurry!*
No! Plenty of Time There Isn't!!
Yes!!! / Till *Tom* stops ringing.
No artifice . . . *a Max Reinhardt nun!*

(*Sebastian appears.*)

Sebastian

Gentlemen
I must leave you a minute . . .

(*Sebastian vomits hugely into the room.*)

The wines were too various
It was neither the *quality* nor the *quantity*
It was *the mixture*
Grasp that
And you have the root of the matter
To understand all is to forgive all . . .

(*And disappears . . .*)

Ryder

The next day
My room is full of flowers . . .
The 'gentleman' from last night had left a note . . .

Sebastian

'I am very contrite
Aloysius won't speak to me until he sees I am forgiven

So please come to luncheon today
Sebastian Flyte.'

FOUR

Ryder walks into a luncheon party . . . rich birds of prey.

Ryder

He is peeling a plover's egg.

(*Sebastian peeling a plover's egg with a menial holding nest full of . . .*)

Sebastian

I've just counted them
There are five each and two over
So I'm having the two *over*
I'm unaccountably *hungry* today!
I'm also drugged up
And have begun to believe the whole of yesterday was *a dream.*
Please don't wake me up.

(*Ryder takes a plover's egg.*
    Both peel and eat plover's eggs as they fall in thrall to each other.)

Ryder

And in an instant I am drugged too.

(*Into this drugged state, Anthony Blanche arrives.*)

Blanche

Well, *hello!*

(*He snatches the plover's eggs.*)

Hurrah p-p-plover's eggs
The first this year
Where did you get them?

15

Sebastian

Mummy sends them from Brideshead
They always lay early for her

Blanche

Lady Marchmain.
Even *p-p-plovers* do her bidding.

Ryder

Hello.
I'm Charles Ryder

Blanche

Hello, Charles Ryder!
Anthony Blanche!
The Oxford *byword* of *iniquity*
I *do* think it is perfectly *brilliant* of Sebastian to have
discovered *you*
What an unexpected t-t-treat!!!
I want you to leave with *me* . . .

(*A slight but steely competition for Charles as . . .*)

Sebastian

Have some more Cointreau, Charles.

Ryder

I think I'll stay.

(*Blanche disappears . . .*
    Something connects. Something happens . . .)

Sebastian

I must go to the Botanical Gardens

Ryder

Why?

Sebastian

To see the ivy.

(*And disappears.*)

Ryder
It's a dream
And I don't want to wake up . . .

FIVE

And is discovered by . . .

Blanche
Charles Ryder!
I have discovered where you l-l-*lurk*
and have come down to your *burrow*
to ch-chivvy you out like *a stoat*!
I'm taking you to d-d-dinner . . .

(*Looks around.*
Hones in on . . .)

I say
These little drawings
Who are they by?

Ryder
Me

Blanche
They're
Exquisite

Ryder
Are they?

Blanche
Utterly exquisite!
Why are they practically h-h-*hidden away* . . .?

(*Sebastian arrives . . .*)

(*To Sebastian.*) You're an artist.
You know Charles is an artist?

Look . . .
He draws like – a young Ingres

(*Sebastian has Aloysius, his teddy bear . . . who
inspects the drawings too.*)

Sebastian
Yes.
Aloysius draws very prettily too
But, of course, he's rather more *modern*.

Charles . . .
Oxford has become *most* peculiar suddenly.
Since last night it has been *pullulating* with *women*.
You're to come away at once, out of danger.

Ryder
Where are we going?

Sebastian
To Brideshead.

SIX

Ryder
A cloudless day in June twenty years ago . . .

(*English countryside sounds.
An early vintage car drives . . .*)

Sebastian and I
In a borrowed, open, two-seater Morris Cowley . . .
A turn in the drive . . .

(*And he's there.*)

A new and secret landscape opens before me . . .
We're at the head of a valley
Below us
A mile distant

18

Grey and gold among the green
The dome and columns of an old house . . .

Sebastian
Brideshead.

(*Beat.*)

Well . . .?

(*Ryder falls in thrall to Brideshead, stares at . . .*)

Ryder
What a place to live in!

Sebastian
You must see the garden and the fountain.
And . . .
There's someone I want you to meet.
. . .

Ryder
At the open window
Fast asleep
A rosary in her hands

Sebastian
Nanny . . . wake up!

Nanny (*wakes up somewhere, as Sebastian kisses her*)
Well – this is a surprise.
Who's this?
I don't think I know him.

Sebastian
My friend, Charles Ryder.

Nanny
Julia's here for the day
You must have just missed her.
It's the Conservative Women.
Her Ladyship was to have done them

But she's poorly in London.
Julia won't be long
She's leaving for *London* immediately after her speech
Before *the tea.*

Sebastian
I'm afraid we won't see her.

Ryder
But I should like to.

Sebastian
Well, you can't
Nanny Hawkins is what we're here for.

Nanny
Now what's the news?
Studying hard at your books?

Sebastian
Not very, I'm afraid, Nanny.

Nanny
Cricketing all day long like your brother!
He's not been here since Christmas
But he'll be here for the Agricultural I expect.
Ring the bell, dear
And we'll have some tea.
I usually go down to Mrs Chandler
But we'll have it up here today.
My usual girl has gone to London with the others.
The new one is just up from the village.
She didn't know *anything* at first
But she's coming along nicely . . .
Ring the bell.

(*A household bell rings.*)

Sebastian
Poor Nanny

She does have such a dull life.
Let's go drink wine under the elm trees!

I've a good mind to bring Nanny to Oxford to live
with me . . .
Only she'd always be trying to send me to church . . .

We must go . . .

Ryder
Am I not going to be allowed to see any more of the
house?

Sebastian
It's all shut up.

(*Beat.*)

Well . . . come and look if you want to . . .

Ryder
His mood had changed since the wine.

Sebastian
There's nothing to see
here's the chapel . . .

(*Sebastian genuflects. Ryder is surprised.*)

Ryder
You're Roman Catholic?

Sebastian
Yes.
Didn't you know?

Ryder
No
Your own private chapel . . .?

Sebastian
It was Papa's wedding present to Mummy
It's apparently a *monument of art nouveau* . . .

(*And they look . . .*)

Ryder
   Golly

Sebastian
   Now, if you've seen enough . . .

Ryder
   Leaving . . .
   We pass a closed Rolls-Royce driven by a chauffeur.
   In the back
   A vague girlish figure who looks round at us through
   the window . . .

   (*Young Julia lit, looks round from a chair . . .*)

Julia
   Light one for me, would you?

Sebastian
   Julia.

Ryder
   Julia.

Sebastian
   We just got away in time.

   (*Beat.*)

   I'm not going to have you get mixed up with the family.
   All my life they've been taking things away from me.
   If they once get hold of you with their charm
   They'll make you their friend not mine and I won't let
   them.

   (*Beat.*)

   I'm sorry
   I'm afraid that wasn't very nice.
   Brideshead often has that effect on me.

SEVEN

Ryder in to Blanche . . .
  Beat.

Ryder
  Tell me about the Marchmains.

Blanche
  Ch-ch-children.

  (*And, somehow, their portraits . . .*)

  Brideshead . . . 'Bridey' . . . eldest and heir . . .
  He's like something out of a cave that's been sealed for
  centuries . . .
  A face as though an Aztec sculptor had attempted a
  portrait of Sebastian . . .
  A learned bigot
  A ceremonious b-b-barbarian
  A snow-bound lama, well, anything you like . . .

  Lady Julia
  Well, you've seen her in all the papers
  Our most d-d-dazzling debutante!
  A face of flawless Florentine quattrocento beauty
  Smart as her mother . . .
  And both she and mother
  Hoping to make a magnificent and appropriate
  marriage . . .

  Sebastian of course . . .
  He was a complete little *bitch* at school
  He was the only boy who was *never* b-b-beaten
  And never had spots
  Not one!
  And of course as you are discovering in *great detail*
  I hear
  utterly charming

There's a girl still in the schoolroom . . .
(*On the very edge of memory . . .*) *Cordelia.*
Nothing known
Except her governess went mad and drowned herself
long ago . . .

Ryder

The parents?

Blanche

Ah . . . it's when you get to the parents the
b-b-bottomless pit opens.
My dear, *such* a pair!!!
D-d-daddy is Lord Marchmain
Little *fleshy* but *very* handsome
A *magnifico*
A voluptuary
Byronic
Bored
Infectiously slothful
And . . .
Forced to live in Venice . . .
Positively the last historic authentic case of someone
being hounded out of society . . .
Because
Mummy
Lady Marchmain,
Very very beautiful
No artifice a Max Reinhardt nun!
Voice quiet as a prayer and as powerful
She won't give him a divorce because she's Roman
Catholic
And soooo pious . . .
She has somehow convinced the world Lord Marchmain
is a monster

Ryder

How?

Blanche
How indeed?
How *does* she do it?
You would th-th-think the old reprobate had *tortured* her
Flung her out of doors
Roasted stuffed and *eaten* her children
Gone frolicking in all the flowers of Sodom and Gomorrah
Instead of what?
Begetting four *splendid* children by her
Then simply *leaving* her after the war . . .
A brave cavalry officer mounting his horse and galloping away . . .
Handing over Brideshead *and* Marchmain House to *her*
All the money she can p-p-possibly spend
While he sits in Venice with a personable middle-aged *person* of the theata
Shunned by *everybody*!!!

She has a small gang of enslaved prisoners and *I*
believe she sucks their blood . . . you can see the
t-t-toothmarks all over poor Adrian Porson's shoulders
when he is bathing!!!

So you see with such a murky past . . .
There's really v-v-very little left for poor Sebastian to
do except be sweet and charming
So you mustn't blame him if at times he seems a little
insipid and anaemic . . . Mummy's a vampire
With God and Right on her side . . .
And you must be t-t-terribly on your guard against her,
Charles . . .

EIGHT

Oxford.

Finding scant loose change in pockets . . .

Ryder
Sebastian!
I've *already* run *completely* out of money.

Sebastian
You spend money like a *bookie.*

Ryder
It all goes *with* you on *you*!
How do *you* manage?

Sebastian
It's all done by lawyers
And I suppose they embezzle a lot
Anyway I never seem to get much.
Of course, Mummy would give me anything I ask for.

Ryder
Then why don't you ask her for a *proper* allowance?

Sebastian
Oh, Mummy likes everything to be *a present.*
She's so sweet.
I'll see you after the long vac.

(*They say goodbye.*)

NINE

London.

Ryder
I'm at home   with my father

Ryder Senior

You are here for long?

Ryder

I'm not quite sure, Father

Ryder Senior

It's a *very* long vacation
In my day we used to go on *reading parties*
In mountainous areas . . .

Ryder

I thought of putting in some time at an art school . . .

Ryder Senior

My dear boy you'll find them all shut.
In my day . . . there was an institution called
'a sketching club'
I expect they still go on.
You might try that.

Ryder

One of the problems of the vacation is the money,
Father

You see I've run rather short

Ryder Senior

Yes?

Ryder

In fact I don't know how I'm going to get through the
next two months . . .

Ryder Senior

Well, I'm the worst person to come to for advice
I've never been 'short' as you so painfully call it . . .
And yet what else could you say . . .?
Hard up?
Penurious?
Embarassed?

Stony broke?
In Queer Street!!
On / the rocks . . .

Ryder

Then what do you suggest my doing?

Ryder Senior

Your cousin Melchior was imprudent with his
investments.
Got into a *very queer street*.
He went to Australia

(*He roars with delight.*)

Ryder

I'd not seen my father so gleeful
Since he found two pages of *second*-century papyrus
Between the leaves of a *Lombardic* breviary.

(*Hayter appears.*)

Ryder Senior

Hayter, I've dropped my book.

Ryder

Father – you surely don't want me to spend the whole
vacation here with you?

Ryder Senior

Eh?

Ryder

Won't you find it rather a bore having me at home for
so long?

Ryder Senior

I trust I should not betray such an emotion even if I
felt it.
Stay as long as you find it convenient.

(*He reads his book . . .*
  Ryder hates his father.
  Until . . .)

What is it, Hayter?

Hayter
  Telegram, sir.
  For Mr Charles

Sebastian
  'Gravely injured.
  Come at once.
  Sebastian.'

(*Ryder leaps to . . .*)

Ryder
  The train.

Train (*seems to say . . .*)
  Too late
  Too late
  He's dead
  He's dead

TEN

Brideshead train station.
  Steam train sounds . . .

Ryder
  You must be Julia

Julia (*in Sebastian's voice . . .*)
  You're Mr Ryder?
  I'm to drive you.
  (*Then , , , in her own voice.*) You're Mr Ryder?
  I'm to drive you.

29

Ryder

How is he?

Julia

He's fine
He's cracked a bone in his ankle so *small*
It doesn't have *a name*
He's been making the most *enormous* fuss
He tried to make *me* stay with him!
He's been *maddeningly* pathetic
He agreed to try *you*.

Ryder

How did he do it?

Julia

Playing croquet!
He *lost* his temper
And tripped over *a hoop*.

(*We see this somewhere as . . .*)

Ryder

She *so much* resembled Sebastian.
I *knew* her
And she did not know me

(*Her eyes on the road, he watches her.*)

Her sex is the palpable difference between the familiar
and the strange.
It seems to fill up the space between us.

(*She hands him a carton of cigarettes.*)

Julia

Light one for me, will you?

(*He puts a cigarette in his mouth. Lights it.*)

Ryder

I felt her to be *especially* female . . .

As I take the cigarette from my lips
And put it in hers

Julia
Thank you

(*She smokes. He watches.*)

Ryder
I catch a thin bat's squeak of sexuality
Inaudible to anyone but me . . .

(*A hobbling Sebastian . . .*)

Julia
Here's the *wounded soldier* . . .

Ryder
I thought you were *dying*!

Sebastian
I thought I was, too!
I'm in *terrible* pain

(*Beat.*)

Do you think if you asked him
Wilcox would give us champagne?

Julia
You seem to let him boss you about a good deal.
You shouldn't.
It's very bad for him.

Ryder
I don't think your sister cares for me

Sebastian
I don't think she cares for anyone much.
That's why I love her.

Ryder
Do you?

Sebastian

She's so like me.

Ryder

Is she?

(*Ryder and Julia regard one another . . .*)

I look and see a brilliant beautiful *terrifying* girl

Julia

I look and see – a – boy

(*Vanishes.*)

Sebastian

We'll have a splendid time *alone.*

(*Birdsong.*
    Summer insects . . .)

Ryder

I believe myself very near heaven
Those languid summer days at Brideshead . . .
If this house were *mine*
I'd never live anywhere else

Sebastian

But you see, Charles
It isn't mine.
Usually
It's full of *ravening beasts*
If it could only always be like this
Summer!
The fruit *ripe*
And Aloysius in a good temper . . .

Ryder

It is *thus* I like to remember Sebastian . . .
in the old nurseries . . . sitting on the threadbare
flowered carpet

The toy-cupboard empty about us . . .
And
Nanny Hawkins stitching complacently in the corner.

Ryder
I *adore* the dome.

Sebastian
Oh Charles, don't be such a *tourist*

Ryder
Is it by Inigo Jones?
It looks later

Sebastian
What does it matter *when* it was built
If it's *pretty*?

Ryder
It's the sort of thing I like to know.

This fountain is extraordinary.

Sebastian
Is it?
Here. I found these in a cupboard.
A box of paints . . .
Mummy bought them a year ago.

(*Ryder opens the paintbox . . .
Something happens . . .*)

Someone told her that 'you can only appreciate the beauty
Of the world by trying to paint it'.

Ryder
Really?

Sebastian
She tried but *everything* came out khaki

(*He laughs.*)

Here
Draw it.
Paint it.
On the garden-room wall.
You know you want to.

(*And, as everywhere new great splashes of colour . . .
    Sebastian vanishes . . .*)

Ryder
It seems as though I was being given a brief spell of
What I had never known . . .
Colour.

Nanny
A pair of children the two of you.

Ryder
A happy childhood.

Nanny
You're one as bad as the other.

Ryder
Its toys – are silk shirts and liqueurs and cigars
And – architecture and *art*

(*Beat.*)

And its 'naughtiness' . . .
High in the catalogue of grave sins . . .?

Nanny
Is that what they teach you at college?

Sebastian (*with glasses, a bottle of wine somewhere*)
Wilcox says a lot of the old wine wants drinking up.
I've found a book on wine-tasting . . .
Shall we try a bottle from *every* bin . . .

(*Reads . . .*)

'Warm the glass slightly at a candle . . .'

(*And then, in stereo . . .*)

Fill it a third high
swirl the wine round
nurse in the hands
hold to the light
breathe it
sip it
fill the mouth with it
roll it over the tongue
ring it on the palate like a coin on a counter . . .
tilt head back
let it trickle down the throat . . .

Ryder
It is a little shy wine like a gazelle

Sebastian (*drunk*)
Like a leprechaun

Ryder
Dappled in a *tapestry* meadow

Sebastian (*drunker*)
Like a *flute* by still water

Ryder
And this is a *very wise* old wine

Sebastian (*very drunk*)
A prophet in *a cave*

Ryder
This is a necklace of pearls on a white neck

Sebastian (*very very drunk*)
This is like – a swan

Ryder
This is like the last unicorn . . .

Sebastian
Ought we to be drunk *every* night?

Ryder
Yes, I think so

Sebastian
I think so too.

Ryder
And so we are . . . until the ravening beasts arrived . . .

(*Various ravening beasts arrive . . .*)

Cordelia
Sebastian Sebastian Sebastian Sebastian!!!!

Bridey
Jessup send Wilcox to tell Jupp to draw my bath early
but don't lay out my evening duds yet I need to go to
the stables and supervise Thunderer's spavin!!

Nanny (*joining the ravening hordes as . . .*)
Ring the bell for tea, dears . . .
The new girl from the village is not bringing in the
library tea!
I'm sorry to say she's not ready yet to be trusted with
the Spode

Sebastian
Oh God . . .
Cordelia.

Cordelia
I *guessed* you were here!!!

Sebastian
Go away, Cordelia.

Cordelia

Why?

Sebastian

We've got no clothes on.

Cordelia

You're Decent.
IcamedownwithBridey
AndstoppedtoseeFrancesXavierhe'smypigthenwe
had lunchthentheshowFrancesXaviergotaspecial
mention*Darling*Sebastianhow'syourpoorfoot?

Sebastian

Say how d'you do to Mr Ryder

Cordelia

Oh sorry, how d'you do?
Bridey'sverysoutodayhedidn'twantmetohavedinner
withyoubutIfixedhim
Come on, make yourself decent . . .

Ryder

And *Bridey* . . .

Sebastian

Oh *God*, Bridey . . .!

Bridey

I am so sorry to miss so much of your visit
You are being looked after properly?
I hope Sebastian is seeing to the wine?
Wilcox is apt to be rather *grudging*
You are fond of wine?
I wish *I* were
It is such a bond with other men
I tried to get drunk once
Didn't enjoy it

Cordelia

I *like* wine.

Bridey

Cordelia's last report said she was not only the *worst* girl in the school,

But the worst there had *ever* been in the memory of the *oldest* nun.

Cordelia

Idon'tbelieveourBlessedLadycarestwo *hoots* WhetherIputmy*gym*shoesontheleftortherightofmy *dancing*shoes

Bridey

Our Lady cares about *obedience*

Sebastian

Bridey, don't be pious

We have an *atheist* among us

Ryder

Agnostic.

Bridey

Really?

Is there much of that at your college?

Cordelia

I'llprayforyouCharles

Sebastian

'I'll pray for you, *Mr Ryder*'

Cordelia

I'llprayforyou*Mr/Ryder*

Bridey

'Agnostic'! Well well!

Sebastian

I must escape!

I think you'd better come with me to Venice

(*Bridey and Cordelia vanish . . .*)

We shall live on Papa when we get there.
As 'the Awful Lawyers' pay for my first class and
sleeper
We can both travel third for that

ELEVEN

Venice sounds, colours as . . .

Sebastian
Papa. Charles.
Charles. Cara.

(*Handshakes etc.*
Then awkward beat . . .)

Lord Marchmain
And how do you plan your time here?
Bathing or sightseeing?

Ryder
S*ome* sightseeing anyway

Lord Marchmain
Cara will like that
Cara is your *hostess* here
You can't do both you know
Once you go to the Lido
You play backgammon
You get caught at the bar
You get stupefied by the sun
Stick to the churches

Sebastian
Charles is very keen on painting

Lord Marchmain
Yes?
Yes?
Any particular Venetian painter?

Ryder (*wildly*)
Bellini . . .

Lord Marchmain
Yes? Which?

(*Beat.*)

Ryder
I'm afraid I didn't know there were two of them.

Lord Marchmain (*very pleased to say* . . .)
Three to be precise.
In the great ages painting was very much a *family*
business
Is painting very much in your family?

Ryder
Not at all.
And I don't have terribly much / of a family . . . just a
father . . .

Lord Marchmain (*to Sebastian* . . .)
How did you leave England?

Sebastian
It has been lovely

Lord Marchmain
Has it?
Has it?
It has been my *tragedy* that I *abominate* the English
countryside.
Disgraceful thing to inherit great responsibilities
And be *entirely* indifferent to them
I am *all t*he Socialists would have me be.

(*Beat. Without conviction.*)

Well, my elder son will change all that!

Cara

Vittoria Corombona has asked us all to her ball on
Sunday

Lord Marchmain

That is *very* kind of her.
You know I do not dance.

Sebastian

He's rather a poppet isn't he?

Ryder

The fortnight passes quickly and sweetly
I am drowning in honey

Lord Marchmain

There is nothing quite like a Venetian crowd
The city is crawling with anarchists
But

(*Lord Marchmain and Cara share a fun joint memory.*)

An *American* woman.

Cara

With *bare shoulders*

Lord Marchmain

Tried to *sit* here the other night
They *drove* her away

Cara

Coming to *stare* at her
Like circling gulls coming back and back to her

Lord Marchmain

Until she *left*!

Ryder

I have . . .
A confused memory of fierce sunlight on the sands
Cool marble interiors

Water lapping everywhere
Painted ceilings

(*They all look up . . .*)

Lord Marchmain
Titian
Tintoretto
Fumiano
Er . . . Charles

Ryder
This is Fumiano!
Churches
All the churches

(*And the space is flooded with religiosity . . .*)

Worshippers / Priests / Nuns / Sightseers / Various
Salvete Domin / um
Salvete Omnes Dom / inum

(*Everyone but Ryder makes some sort of religious obeisance.*)

Sebastian
Oh dear its very *difficult* being Catholic

Ryder
Does it make much difference to you?

Sebastian
Of course. All the time.

Ryder
Are you struggling against temptation?

Sebastian
Always.

Ryder
You don't seem *much* more virtuous than me.

Sebastian
Charles . . .
I'm *very much* wickeder . . .

Ryder
Do they try and make you believe an awful lot of
nonsense?

Sebastian
Is it nonsense?
I wish it were
It sometimes sounds terribly sensible to me

Ryder
You can't *seriously* believe it

Sebastian
It's a lovely idea

Ryder
But you can't believe things because they're a lovely
idea

Sebastian
But I *do*. That's how I *believe*.
Don't be a bore, Charles
Aloysius and I want to enjoy this *ridiculous* ceiling!

Ryder
Night fishing for scampi in the shallows of Chioggia

Sebastian
The phosphorescent wake of a little ship

Ryder
The lantern swinging in the prow

Sebastian
And the *net* coming up full of *weed* and *sand* and
floundering fishes . . .

(*And they head drinkwards as . . .*)

Ryder
And
One particular conversation towards the end of my
visit . . .

Cara
I think you are very fond of Sebastian.

Ryder
Why, certainly.

Cara
I know of these *romantic friendships* of the English
and Germans.
I think they are good if they do not go on too long.
In England it comes when you are almost men

Ryder
Yes

Cara
I think I *like* that!
Better to have that love for a *boy* than a *girl*.
Alex had it for his wife.
Do you think he loves me?

Ryder
Really Cara / . . . I couldn't

Cara
He does not.
But not the *littlest* piece.
Then why does he stay with me . . .?

(*Ryder daren't say.*)

I *protect* him from Lady Marchmain!!!
He *hates* her
He is a *volcano* of hate
He cannot breathe the same air as she!
He will not touch a hand which may have touched hers

We have guests . . .
I see him thinking . . .
'Have they perhaps just come from Brideshead?'
'Are they a link between me and her whom I hate?'
But seriously, with my heart, this is how he thinks!
She has done nothing . . .
except to be loved by someone who was not grown-up.
He can scarcely be happy with Sebastian because he is
her son but
Sebastian hates her too

Ryder

I'm sure you're wrong ab / out that

Cara

My dear boy, you are very young
They are full of hate
Hate of *themselves*
When someone hates with all their energy
It is something in themselves they are hating.
Alex is hating all the illusions of boyhood . . .
Innocence . . .
Sebastian hasn't grown up . . .
Sebastian is in love with his childhood.
His teddy bear . . .
His nanny . . .
That will make him very unhappy . . .

(*Beat. Cara watches the boats passing on the water.*)

Sebastian drinks too much.

Ryder

I suppose we both do

Cara

I see it in the way he drinks
It is not your way.
He will be a drunkard if someone does not come to
stop him

Alex was nearly a drunkard when he met me
It is in the blood.

(*And vanishes . . .*)

TWELVE

Ryder drawing, Sebastian and Aloysius. Sebastian drinking . . .

Ryder
Autumn term.

Sebastian
I feel precisely one hundred years old.
Oh Charles, what has happened since last term?
I feel so *old*!

Ryder
I feel *middle-aged*.
That is *infinitely* worse.
I believe we have had all the fun we can expect here

Sebastian
Anthony Blanche has gone down
He's taken a flat in *Munich*
He's formed an attachment to a pretty *policeman* there.

Ryder
My drawings are *worthless*.

Sebastian
Are they?
Aloysius, what do *you* think of Charles' drawings . . .?

(*Aloysius inspects Ryder's work . . .*
    Ryder is just a little irritated.)

Ryder
We're keeping too much to our own company this
term . . .

People don't like it . . .

(*Lady Marchmain appears.*
 Ryder and Sebastian scramble.)

Lady Marchmain
Sebastian. Darling!

Sebastian
Mummy! Darling!

Lady Marchmain
I thought I *must* spend a week in Oxford . . .
Spend time with my darling Sebastian and his *friends*.

Sebastian
Mummy . . .
This is Charles Ryder . . .

Lady Marchmain
Charles.
You have been such a *good kind* friend to my darling
boy . . .
All his *host* of friends seem reduced to *one* . . . yourself.
I welcome you as Sebastian's dearest friend.
I hope you will become *my friend* also . . . ?

Ryder
I hope so / too.

Lady Marchmain
Darling . . . Monsignor Bell is *terribly* keen for you to
have a little *talk* with him . . . I understand from him
that you have made rather a *bad* start last year
And have been *noticed* . . .

(*Beat.*)

Indulge me, darling, and trundle along now to the
Monsignor . . .

(*Beat.*)

Charles can entertain me . . .

(She has a book . . .)

Charles . . . I am making a memorial book about my
brother Ned

(Opens it.)

Who was the last of my three brothers

(She uses the book as a lure.)

All lost in the war . . .
Ned killed between Mons and Passchendaele . . .

(A tragic photograph.)

Ryder

I'm so sorry

Lady Marchmain

Thank you Charles . . . Charles . . .
I am seeking outside advice about his papers
From Mr Samgrass . . .
Do you know Mr Samgrass . . . /
Who I think should become
Sebastian's tutor . . .

(She has coerced Sebastian away.
*As Ryder and Lady Marchmain look through her
book . . .)*

Sebastian

You and Mummy seem very thick . . .

Ryder

Nonsense.

Sebastian

It's not non / sense . . .

Lady Marchmain

Charles . . . My Oxford week is almost at an end!
Sebastian darling . . . Mr Samgrass is *expecting* you . . .

(*Sebastian and Charles again separated.*)

Charles, I shall miss you too much . . .
You must promise me to spend all Christmas vacation
at Brideshead!

(*Lady Marchmain vanishes . . .*)

Ryder
From then on . . .
Sebastian *accelerates* his drinking
And the number of unfortunate incidents *increase*
Exponentially . . . the brushes with the law . . . the
bad / company . . .
Oh Sebastian, so very drunk *again*!!!

Sebastian
Merely *merry*, Charles . . .
Mummy's paid my fine

Ryder
Without *fuss*.

Sebastian
Mummy *never* fusses

Ryder
She *couldn't* have been more charming

Sebastian
Mummy's *always* charming

Ryder
Why do you do this? Why??

Sebastian
I can't explain.
Charles . . .
Come to Brideshead for Christmas
Please.

THIRTEEN

Christmas country bells.

Samgrass
Ryder!
Welcome and Merry Christmas!!

Ryder
Mr Samgrass??!

Samgrass
You find me in *solitary* possession of this *magnificent*
house!
We had a lawn meet of the hounds
All our young friends are *fox-hunting*
Even Sebastian
Very *elegant* in his pink coat!
Our hostess remained at home
Sir Adrian Porson of *course*
Two rather f*orbidding* Magyar cousins
I tried them in German and French
In *neither* tongue are they diverting
Your arrival *emboldens* me to ring for some tea
The party breaks up tomorrow
Lady Julia departs for another party for New Year
And takes the *demi-monde* with her
I shall *miss* the pretty creatures about the house
Particularly Celia . . .
The sister of *Boy Mulcaster*!

Ryder
Positively the earliest sighting of my *ambitious* wife!

Samgrass
Most engaging . . .

Ryder
Celia. Yes. Most engaging.
In a school-monitor-style dress

Samgrass
I can only call *saucy* . . .

Sebastian
Charles!
I'm so profoundly glad you're here!

Lady Marchmain (*vampire grooming*)
We must make a *Catholic* out of Charles!

Ryder
One is never *summoned* for a little talk
It merely *happens*
One finds oneself *alone* / with her

(*And she's got him* . . .)

Sebastian
She's *always* doing it.
I wish to *hell* she wouldn't.

Lady Marchmain
When I married I became very rich.
It used to worry me *terribly*.
The *poor* have always been the favourites of God and
his saints.

Ryder
Well . . . camel, eye of a needle / I suppose . . .

Lady Marchmain
It's very *unexpected*, isn't it?
But the Gospel is a *catalogue* of unexpected things
In the lives of the saints
Animals do the *oddest* things . . .

Ryder
I have no mind for anything
Except Sebastian . . . and . . .
I see him already threatened . . .

Lady Marchmain
Sebastian, come join us . . . Charles and I are *debating*.

Sebastian
You and Charles seem debatable *enough*, Mummy!

Ryder
His days in *Arcadia* are numbered

Lady Marchmain / Samgrass
Sebastian, come sit / with me
I have a proof copy of this new book on Byzantine
Iconography . . .
Sebastian, shall we study for a while?
Sebastian dear! Sebastian . . .

Sebastian
I want to be *let alone*

Ryder
In this time
Sebastian took fright . . .

Sebastian
I am sick of being *grateful* to Mr Samgrass
I can't stand this any more.
Let's *run*, Charles!

FOURTEEN

Ryder
I thought we'd escaped
but
when he was cheerful and happy now
it was usually because he was *drunk*

(St Mary's chime, to which . . .)

Sebastian

'Green arse, Samgrass,
Samgrass green arse . . .'

Ryder

I drink less
He drinks *more*
A succession of disasters come on him
So swiftly
And with such unexpected violence
It's hard to say *when* exactly I know my friend is in
deep trouble

(Beat.)

I know it well enough at Brideshead
in the Easter vacation . . .

(Sebastian lurking . . .)

Sebastian

Haven't they brought the cocktails yet?

Ryder

Where have you been?

Sebastian

Up with Nanny.

Ryder

Liar.
You've been drinking / somewhere

Sebastian

My cold's worse today

Ryder

Go to bed.
I'll say your cold's worse
And don't have any more of *this*

(*They wrestle over drinks.*)

Sebastian
You put that / down

Ryder
Don't be an *ass*, Sebastian.
You've had *enough*.

Sebastian
What the *devil's* it got to do with *you*?
You're only a *guest* in this house!
Stop *spying* on me for my mother!
I drink what I want in my own house!

(*Beat.*
   Sebastian weaves off. Julia arrives.)

Ryder
Julia . . . Sebastian's drunk.

Julia
What a *bore* he is!
Will he be alright for dinner?

Ryder
No.

Julia
Well you must *deal* with him.
Does he often do this?

Ryder
Lately, yes.

Julia
How *very* boring.

Ryder
Lady Marchmain . . .
Sebastian's cold has come on rather badly
He's gone to bed and says he doesn't / want anything.

Lady Marchmain
Poor Sebastian.
He'd better have a hot whisky.
I'll go have a look / at him.

Julia (*half rising*)
Don't, Mummy.
Don't, Cordelia! /
I'll go.

Cordelia
I *already* called for him and I think / he's *very drunk*!

Ryder / Julia
Cordelia!

Cordelia
'Marquis's Son Unused to Wine!'
'Model Student's Career Threatened!'

Lady Marchmain
Charles, is this true?

Ryder
Yes.

(*Sebastian arrives.*)

Sebastian
Come to apologise

Lady Marchmain
Sebastian dear, do go back to your room
We can talk about it in the morning

Sebastian
Not to *you*.
To *Charles*.
I was *bloody* to him
And he's *my* guest and my only friend and I was
bloody to him.

Ryder
It's time you were in bed.

Sebastian
Why do you take their side against me?
I *knew* you would if I let you *meet* them.
Why do you *spy* on me?

Ryder
Where are you going?

Sebastian
London I suppose
I shall go on running away
As far and as fast as I can
You can hatch up any plot you like with my mother
I shan't come back.

(*And he disappears.*)

Lady Marchmain
Charles, I look on you very much as one of *ourselves.*
Sebastian loves you
I slept very little last night . . .
I kept thinking
He was so unhappy . . .
I have been praying and wondering . . .
I don't want him to be *ashamed*.

Ryder
He's ashamed of being *unhappy.*

Lady Marchmain
This has all happened before!

Ryder
No. Last night was quite new to me.

Lady Marchmain
Not with Sebastian
With his father . . .

Drunk in *just that way*!
And the *running away*
He ran away from me too, Charles!
It's too pitiful
You've got to help him.

Ryder

I can't.

Lady Marchmain

Charles . . .
I wonder if you have seen my brother's book
It's just come out
May I give you a copy?
When Ned was killed
And the telegram came
As I knew it would
I thought
'Now it's my son's turn to do what Ned can never do
now . . .'
I was alone then.
Sebastian was just going to Eton . . . /
If you read this you'll understand . . .

Ryder

I think
She's *planned* this parting.

Lady Marchmain

I prayed for you, too, in the night

Ryder

I'm old enough to know an attempt had been made to
suborn me
And young enough to find it agreeable . . .

(*Goes to join Sebastian as . . .*)

Cordelia

Will you be seeing Sebastian, Charles?

Please give him my special love.
Will you remember . . . my *special* love??

Sebastian
Did you have a little *talk* with Mummy?

Ryder
Yes.

Sebastian
Have you gone over to her side?

Ryder
No, I'm with *you*.
Sebastian *contra mundum.*

FIFTEEN

Sebastian
There's a *plot* going on.
Mummy wants me to live with *Monsignor Bell.*
I am *not* going to live with Monsignor Bell.
Mummy's very clever / you know.

Lady Marchmain
'I shall be passing through Oxford
I would like to see you alone five minutes before I see
him'

(*And is there, with Ryder . . .*)

What lovely rooms!
Ned had rooms on the garden front
I wanted Sebastian to come here
But my husband was at Christ Church and . . .

(*She's prowling . . .*)

What *lovely* drawings
E*verybody* loves your paintings in the garden room . . .

We shall *never* forgive you if you don't finish them . . .
Is Sebastian drinking too much this term?

Ryder
If he were I shouldn't answer.
As it is . . . I can say no

Lady Marchmain
I believe you.
Thank God.

Ryder
Sebastian you're *hopelessly* drunk.

Sebastian
That's because
Mummy's been visiting you . . .
I can *scent* her all around . . .

Ryder
Have you been drinking by yourself after I've left you?

Sebastian
About *twice* . . .
Perhaps *four* times
It's only when they start *bothering* me
If they'd leave me *alone*

Ryder
You're *contemptible* . . .

(*And loses it.*)

Really
If you're going to do this every time
You see a member of your family
It's *hopeless*!!

Sebastian
Oh yes
I *know*
It's hopeless

Ryder
What do you propose to do?

Sebastian
I shan't do anything.
They'll do it all.

(*And he vanishes.*)

Ryder (*heartbroken*)
And I let him go without *comfort*

(*To Lady Marchmain.*)

You must believe when I said Sebastian was not drinking
I was telling you the truth as I knew it

Lady Marchmain
I know you wish to be a good friend to him

Ryder
That's not what I mean
I believe he has been drunk only two or three times

Lady Marchmain
It's no good, Charles
All you can mean is you have not as much influence or
knowledge of him
As I thought.
I've known drunkards before.
I know their *deceit*.
Love of *truth* is the first thing to go.
You know we are all fond of you
We should miss you so much if you ever stopped
coming to stay
But
I want Sebastian to have all sorts of friends
Monsignor Bell says he *never* mixes with *other* Catholics.
But he *must* know *some*!
It needs a very *strong* faith to stand alone

And Sebastian's isn't strong
He will not be sent down if he goes to live with
the Monsignor
Monsignor says to say how *welcome* you would
always be
There's not room for you in the Old Palace
But I daresay you wouldn't want that yourself.

Ryder
Lady Marchmain
If you want to make him a *drunkard*
That's the way to do it
The idea of his being *watched* will / be *fatal*.

Lady Marchmain
Oh dear
Protestants *always* think Catholic priests are *spies*.

Ryder
I don't mean that.
He *must* feel free.

Lady Marchmain
But he's been free
Up till now
And look at the result

Ryder
That night
Sebastian and I get *deliriously* drunk together.

Sebastian
Contra mundum?

Ryder
Contra mundum.

I see him to the gate
Reel back to my rooms under a starry heaven
And fall asleep in my clothes

I think . . . everything will be like it was before . . .
In the morning . . .
A note from Lady / Marchmain . . .

Lady Marchmain
'My dear Charles
Sebastian left me this morning to join his father abroad
Mr Samgrass has *very* kindly consented to take charge
of him.
They will go together to visit the Levant
Where Mr Samgrass has long been anxious to
investigate a number of Orthodox monasteries.
Sebastian's stay here has not been happy.
When they come home at Christmas I know Sebastian
will want to see you
And so shall we all.
I went to the garden room this morning and was so
very sorry.
Yours sincerely
Teresa Marchmain.'

(*And she vanishes.*)

SIXTEEN

Julia
It is time to speak of Julia . . .

Ryder
It is time to speak of Julia
For many years we are
Ships
Passing in the night

Julia
Until we are *on* a ship *in* the night . . .
And there is no passing one another at all . . .

Ryder

But we remain *strangers*.

Julia

Yes.
I'd made a kind of *note* of you in my mind . . .
As if . . .
Scanning the shelf for a particular book
One will sometimes have one's attention
Caught by another . . .
Take it down
Glance at the title page
And think
'I must read that, too, when I've the time'
replace it
and continue the search.

Ryder

My interest was *keener*
The physical likeness between sister and brother you
see . . .

(*He stands and walks round Julia.*)

In different poses
Under different lights
Every time
Pierced me anew.

Julia

When we ran into one another . . .
I sometimes caught you looking at Sebastian . . .
then at me . . .
at Brideshead . . .
when Sebastian returns from his Grand Tour . . .

(*Lady Marchmain, Cordelia, Ryder, Bridey sit around
bored rigid as . . .*)

Lady Marchmain (*lying*)
Do continue, Mr Samgrass.

Samgrass
And when we reached the top of the pass
We heard the galloping horses behind
And two soldiers rode up and turned us back.
The General had sent them
There was *a band* not a mile ahead!!

Julia
A *band*?
Goodness!!

Lady Marchmain
I suppose the sort of folk music you get in those parts
is very monotonous . . .

Samgrass
Dear Lady Marchmain . . . a band of *brigands*.

Lady Marchmain
Ah . . .

Samgrass
The mountains are full of them

Cordelia (*to Ryder*)
Dododopinchme

Julia
So you never got to wherever it was . . .

Cordelia
Weren'tyouterriblydisappointedSebastian?

Sebastian
Me?
Me?
Oh, I don't think I was there that day, was I, Sammy?

Samgrass
That was the day you were ill.

Sebastian (*like an echo*)
 I was ill
 So I never should have got to wherever it was, should
 I, Sammy?

Samgrass
 Now *this*, Lady Marchmain
 Is the caravan at Aleppo
 That's our Armenian cook Begedbian
 That's me on the pony

Bridey
 That's a *Kurdish* saddle isn't it . . . ?

Samgrass
 That's the tent folded up
 That's a rather tiresome Kurd who *would* follow us
 about . . .

Bridey
 I *knew* it was a Kurdish saddle

Samgrass
 Here I am in Pontus
 Ephesus
 Trebizond . . .
 Al /eppo . . .

 (*Etc. As . . .*)

Cordelia
 Allguidesandruinsandmules.
 No*Sebastian*!*Where'sSebastian*?

Samgrass
 He held the camera
 He became quite an expert, didn't you, Sebastian?

 (*No answer.*)

 There's Sebastian
 On the hotel terrace in Beirut.

Ryder
Isn't that Anthony Blanche . . . ?

Sebastian
We met him by chance in Constantinople.
He lent me a tenner just before S-S-Samgrass came /
panting up . . .

Samgrass
He accompanied us all the way to Beirut, didn't he
Sebastian?

(*No answer.*)

He was quite *delightful* company, wasn't he, Sebastian?

(*No answer.*)

He had a *beard*

Sebastian
and a *very* pretty Jewish boy . . .

(*Family froideur . . .*
   Sebastian takes Ryder aside.)

I made him take off the beard
And suggested to Sammy that *we* go our separate ways
and
As I'm of age and not certified yet . . .

Samgrass
Ah, don't get up, Lady Marchmain . . .
I have a whole lot of photographs of *Constantinople*!

(*Lady Marchmain, Bridey and Julia are trapped.*)

Sebastian
He couldn't have me arrested
Or leave me to starve while *he* was living on *my* money.
Blanche said it was far better to arrange things
amicably . . .

Ryder

And trick your mother.

Sebastian

Yes!
Wasn't I *clever*?
Samgrass is a *terrible crook* . . .

Samgrass

This is the great harbour from the *east* . . .

Sebastian

Hence . . . the most terrific *smoke screen*!
And . . . if you pretend you are the one taking the
photographs . . .
It seems one is *always* where one should be
Doing what one *should*.

Come and tell me about Paris

Cordelia

CanIcometoo?

Ryder

I have rooms in the Ile Saint-Louis . . .
My teachers are terribly *good*
My fellow students terribly *bad*
I'm trying to be a *good* painter
And succeeding only in being a terribly *bad* one.

Cordelia

Charles
ModernArtisall *bosh*isn'tit?

Ryder

Great bosh

Cordelia

Oh I'm so glad
NowIcanargue againstour'art'nunwhosaysthat'we
shouldn'ttrytocriticisewhatwedidn'tunderstand'and say

Ihaditstraightfrom*areal*artist
And snubs to *her.*

Sebastian

Go change for supper, Cordelia.

(*Cordelia exits.*
    No sign of the cocktail tray.
    Footman appears.)

No sign of the cocktail tray, Phelps.

Footman

Mr Wilcox is upstairs with Her Ladyship

Sebastian

Well, never mind . . .
Bring in the cocktail things . . .

Footman

Mr Wilcox has the keys, My Lord . . .

(*Beat.*)

Sebastian

Well then . . . I'll take my bath.

(*And he exits.*)

Bridey

My mother has given orders
No drinks to be left in any of the rooms . . .

Ryder

Is that necessary?

Bridey

I gather *very* necessary
Will *you* have a cocktail, now he's gone upstairs?

Ryder

Bridey . . . It would *choke* me.

Julia

Sebastian has got *tight* again.
It's *too* tedious.

Ryder
It's pretty boring for *him* too.

Julia
Well, it's *his* fault.
Why can't he behave like everyone else?

Ryder
As Sebastian fades and crumbles
Julia . . .
Begins to stand out
Clear and firm . . .

SEVENTEEN

Julia
The aim of *me* and all my friends
is
To be married *soon* and *splendidly*
I see marriage as the beginning of individual existence!

Ryder
She outshines by far all the girls of her age

Julia
I *know* I'm beautiful!
I *know* I shine
I'm a *bright star*!!
But

Ryder
There is the scandal of her father . . .

Society Various
There's a slight inherited *stain* / upon her brightness yes!
She *should* be able to snag a *royal* but / . . . the father?
Roman Catholic . . . not going to *wash*, is it?

Ryder
And a waywardness and wilfulness

In her own way of life
That *deepens* that stain . . .

Julia

wherever I turn
my *religion* stands as a barrier
between *me* and my natural goal
A splendid *English* marriage is usually *Protestant* . . .
My religion seems to me *a dead loss*!
But . . .
if I *apostatise*
I will go to *hell*

Ryder

then
she meets *Rex*

Julia

I think I start being interested in him because I *know*
Mummy would *hate* it

He's *Canadian*

He can fix *anything*

He will drive me *anywhere*

He's lucky with money

He's *big*

He plays golf with the Prince of Wales

He knows Gertie Lawrence!!

And *Augustus John*

He has a Military Cross!!

He's a *war hero*

I hear he has a *gun*

Ryder
He is . . .
Perfectly *wrong*

Julia
In *every way*

Rex
Ma Marchmain doesn't like me

Lady Marchmain
Rex *Mottram* . . . ?

Rex
Well, I'm not asking her to.
It's not *her* I want to marry!
She hasn't got the guts to say openly . . .
'You're not a gentleman . . .
You're an *adventurer* from *The Colonies*.'

Ryder
Rex wants a woman
He wants the best on the market
And he wants her at his own price

Rex
She says

Lady Marchmain
You live in different *atmospheres*, you see . . .

Rex
That's all right
But Julia happens to fancy my atmosphere
Right, Julia?

Julia
I *think* so . . .

Rex
Then she brings up *religion*.

Lady Marchmain

We're Roman Catholics you see / and . . .

Rex

We don't take much account of Catholics in Canada
But that's different
In Europe you've got some very posh Catholics.
All right, Julia can go to church whenever she wants
It doesn't mean two pins to her
But I like a girl to have religion
Then there's my *past*.

Lady Marchmain

We know so *little* about you.

Rex

She knows a sight *too much*!
I've been tied up with someone else for a year or two . . .

Ryder

Brenda Champion!!
Rex is older than her
That is in his favour
That was really the *only* thing in his f-f-favour . . .

Julia

He really wasn't quite the thing *at all*!

Ryder

Of course he could *reel in* Lady Marchmain and Julia
like a couple of salmon!!

Lady Marchmain

Aunt Fanny tells me you made great friends with Mr
Mottram
I'm sure he can't be very nice.

Julia

I don't think he is.
I don't know that I like *nice* people
He's *pursuing* me.

(*To Footman.*) Did Mr Mottram ring up by any chance?

Footman

Oh yes, My Lady, four times.
Shall I put him through when he rings again?

Julia

Yes. No. Say I've gone out.

Rex

'Mr Mottram expects Lady Julia at The Ritz at one-thirty.'

Julia

I won't I simply won't do as he tells me
I'll lunch *at home*
Go shopping
Return at *six* . . .

Footman

Mr Mottram is waiting, My Lady
I've shown him to the library

Julia

Oh Mummy, I can't be bothered with him
Do tell him to go home.

Lady Marchmain

That's not at all kind, Julia.

Julia

Oh Mummy, *must* I see him??
There'll be a *scene* if I do

Lady Marchmain

Nonsense, Julia.
You twist that poor man round your *finger*.

Rex

So she joins me in the library
And comes out an hour later
Engaged to be married!

Julia

Mummy . . . I *warned* you this would happen!

Lady Marchmain

We know nothing about him!
I don't trust him an inch!

Julia

I *warned* you!

Lady Marchmain

I'm sure he'll have very unpleasant children!
I regard him entirely *unsuitable* as your husband
So will *everyone*.

Julia

Damn everyone!
I'm . . . rescuing a fallen man!
I'm . . . *saving* him from *mortal* sin.

Rex

I got hold of her in the library
made love to her that afternoon for the first time
convinced her . . .
there's a *passion* there

Julia

Rex has a – a – *passion*
that discloses the corner of something like it in *me*

(*Beat.*)

It frightened me
But . . .
I wanted it desperately . . .
If only we can be married immediately.

Rex

For *six weeks* she keeps me at arm's length.

Ryder

Then . . .

Julia

I hear you've been at *a weekend*

Rex

Yes

Julia

And *Brenda Champion* has been there too

Rex

Ah, *Brenda Champion* . . .

Ryder

Married but *always* available . . .

Rex

What do you *expect*?

(*Stand-off.*
Rex and Julia look at one another and . . .)

Julia

And *that's* when I fall in love with him!

Rex

Let's get married!
I saw a spanking good royal wedding in Madrid!
I'd like something of that kind for mine
That's one thing your Church can do . . . put on a
good show!

Lady Marchmain

Mr Mott / ram . . .

Rex

Rex, Lady M . . .

Lady Marchmain

Mr . . . Rex . . . A *mixed* marriage must be a very
unostentatious / affair . . .

Rex

How d'you mean, 'mixed'?

Julia

Darling, between a *Protestant* and a *Catholic*.

Rex

Well, if *that's* all, I'll become a Catholic.

Lady Marchmain

It would be *very* wicked to take a step like this without
believing *sincerely.*

Julia

He is *masterly* in his treatment of Mummy . . .

Rex

A man *needs* a religion.
If *your* Church is good enough for *Julia*
It's good enough for *me*.

Lady Marchmain

Very well . . . I will see about having you *instructed*.
I will telephone Father Mackay . . .

Julia

After Rex's third interview . . .
Father Mackay comes to tea with Mother.

Father Mackay

He's the most *difficult* convert I have ever met!
I can't get anywhere near him.
He doesn't seem to have the *least* intellectual curiosity
or *piety*.
I asked him what he meant by prayer
He said

Rex

I don't mean anything.
You tell me.

Father Mackay

I tried to tell him
And he / said

Rex

Right. So much for prayer.
What's the next thing?

Father Mackay

Has Our Lord more than one nature?

Rex

Just as many as you say, Father.

Father Mackay

Suppose the Pope looks up and sees a cloud and says
It's going to rain . . .
would that be bound to happen?

Rex

Oh yes, Father

Father Mackay

But supposing it didn't?

Rex (*thinks for a minute then . . .*)

I suppose it would be sort of raining *spiritually*
Only we were too sinful to see it . . .

Father Mackay

Lady Marchmain . . .
Choose one of the *younger* fathers for this task . . .
I shall be dead *long* before Rex is a Catholic

Julia

Then . . .
A letter from Bridey . . .

Lady Marchmain

Rex, Bridey has been making some enquiries . . .
He says you were married in Montreal to a Miss Sarah
Evangeline Cutler.

Rex

Yes

Lady Marchmain
Who is *still* alive!

Rex
Is she?

Julia
Rex, is this true?

Rex
Sure it's true.
Sally.
I was only a kid.
I *got* my divorce! Back in *1919*.
What's all the rumpus?

Julia
Don't you realise you poor sweet *oaf*
That you *can't* get married as *a Catholic* when you've
another wife alive?

Rex
But I *haven't*!
I was divorced six years ago!

Julia
But you *can't* be divorced as a Catholic

Rex
I wasn't a Catholic when I was divorced!

Lady Marchmain
Didn't Father Mackay *explain* this to you?

Rex
Well I'm damn *busy*
I can't remember *everything* he tells me . . .
Hey now . . .
What about your Italian cousin . . .?
Francesca?
She married twice

Lady Marchmain
She had *an annulment.*

Rex
All right then . . . *I'll* get an annulment
What d'you want me to do?
Who should I see?
Don't you tell me there isn't someone who can't fix this!
All right, to hell
We'll be married in a Protestant church!!

Lady Marchmain
You will not!

Julia
We *will*!

Lady Marchmain
Julia . . . I can *stop* this!

Julia
But, I don't think you will, Mummy
I've been Rex's mistress for some time now
And I shall go on being . . .
Married or not.

Lady Marchmain
Rex, is this true?

Rex
No, damn it, it's not!

Lady Marchmain
I can't go on any more tonight!
I'm utterly exhausted with this!
Someone, anyone!! Help me upstairs!

Julia
I *so* wanted to be his mistress!
Then he wouldn't *need* Brenda Champion!!
I went to Father Mackay

Father . . .
I really *need* to sleep with my future husband . . .

Father Mackay
Ah, child . . .
You must wait until after the nuptials . . .

Julia
Surely, Father Mackay . . .
It can't be wrong to commit a *small* sin *myself*
If it keeps him from a much worse one?

Father Mackay
It *is* wrong, child.

Julia
You are refusing me what I *want*!

Father Mackay
Yes, child.

Julia
What I *need*.

Father Mackay
Yes, child.
And now you had better make your confession

Julia
No thank you
I don't think I want to today

From this moment on . . .
I shut my mind against religion.

(*Beat.*)

Oh Charles, what a squalid wedding!

Ryder
It is an awfully unpopular wedding

Julia
Everyone takes Mummy's side
Everyone always does!
Everyone says I'm behaving *abominably* to her
and
Poor Rex finds he's married –

Rex
A damned outcast!!

Julia
Which was exactly the *opposite* of all he'd wanted

Ryder
It is ten years later that she says this to me
In a storm in the Atlantic.

EIGHTEEN

Easter bells . . .
  Easter hymn . . .

Voices Hunting Various
Weather report says we're in / for a fine day
Jessop, lay out the hunting pink . . . stirrup cup on the
south lawn I think /
Coombs, press my tweeds / I'm not taking that /
piebald / she shies terribly at hedges

Lady Marchmain
Who's hunting?

Cordelia
I am

Julia
Rex is arriving sometime
I'd better stay in to greet him

Bridey

I'm taking that young horse of Julia's
Just to show him the hounds . . .
Sebastian wants to hunt . . .
He can have Tinkerbell
She's been going very nicely this season

Samgrass

Sebastian is in pursuit of the fox
Our little problem is shelved for an hour or two

Ryder

But no, not even for an hour . . .

Sebastian

They've stopped my banking account
I pawned my watch and cigarette case to ensure a
happy Christmas
I've got to come to you for expenses

Ryder

I won't
You know perfectly well I can't

Sebastian (*hunting flask* . . .)

You see?
Empty
I can't be trusted that far.

(*Beat.*)

It's they who are mad, not me.
Now you can't refuse me money.

Ryder

Here

Sebastian

More

Ryder

Here

Sebastian
To the hunt!

Ryder
And I watch him mount and trot off after his brother and sister

Bridey
A day's hunting will put all that *right*

Lady Marchmain
My heart is quite light thinking of Sebastian out with the hunt.

Julia
Mummy, do look at Rex's present

(*A bejewelled tortoise . . .*)

It's –

Ryder
A small tortoise

(*They all examine it . . .*)

Julia
With my initials set in diamonds in the living shell

Lady Marchmain
Dear me!
I wonder if it eats the same sort of things
as an *ordinary* tortoise

Samgrass
What will you do when it's dead?

(*Beat.*)

Will you have another tortoise fitted in to the shell?

Ryder
It's touching to see the *faith* everybody puts in the value of hunting . . .

All is *roseate* with hope
Until . . .

Cordelia
Sebastian's in disgrace
He's just rung to be fetched from South Twining

Ryder
South Twining?
Who lives there?

Cordelia
He was speaking from *the hotel*
Goodness he *did* get lost!

Ryder
He arrived home two-thirds drunk

(*Sebastian before Lady Marchmain.*
  They regard one another until . . .)

Lady Marchmain
Dear boy
How nice to see you looking so well again.
Your day in the open has done you good.
The drinks are on the table.
Do help yourself.

Sebastian
Thanks.
I will.

(*And drinks, as his mother watches him.*)

Lady Marchmain
Charles . . .
Did you give Sebastian money?

Ryder
Yes

Lady Marchmain
Knowing how he was likely to spend it

Ryder
Yes

Lady Marchmain
I don't understand it
I simply don't understand how anyone can be so
callously wicked

(*Ryder says nothing.*)

I'm not going to reproach you
God knows its not for me to reproach anyone
Any failure in my children is my failure
But I don't understand it
I don't understand how you can have been so nice in
so many ways
And then do something so wantonly cruel
I don't understand how we all liked you so much.
Did you hate us all the time?
I don't understand how we deserved it.

Ryder
And she casts me, the *serpent*, out of Eden . . .

Cordelia
'Dear Charles
I amwritingyouthis*secret letter*
I heardallaboutyourdisgrace
Itooamindisgrace!!
IsneakedWilcox'skeysandgotwhiskyforSebastianand
gotcaught.
He did seem to want it so.
Therewasanawfulrow
Julia'stortoisehasdisappeared.
I am well.
Cordelia.'

Ryder
    I shall never go back
    I said
    I have left behind illusion
    Henceforth
    I live in a world of *three* dimensions
    With the aid of my five senses . . .

    (*And exits the space.*)

    End of Act One.

Act Two

ONE

A wild drunken party.
  Someone is dancing relentlessly . . .
  Ryder finds Anthony Blanche in the throng . . .

Ryder
  Blanche . . .
  You must help me!

Blanche
  Must I, Ch-Ch-Charles . . .?

Ryder
  Please.
  Lady Marchmain is very ill.
  I need to find Sebastian . . . and . . .
  Bring him home while there's still time . . .

Blanche
  Sebastian?
  I've had nothing to do with him for *y-y-years*!
  He came to live with *me* in Marseille when *you* threw
  him over
  And really
  It was as m-m-much as I could *stand*!
  My dear, he'd become such a *sot*
  Sip, sip, *sip*, like a dowager
  All day long
  And so *sly*
  I was always *missing* things
  Things I rather *liked* . . .
  Two suits!
  Of course I didn't *know* it was Sebastian

87

There *were* some queer fish in and out of my little
apartment of *course* . . .
But . . .

Ryder

In Marseille?

Blanche

Eventually I found the pawnshop where he was
popping them
And *then* discovered he hadn't got the decency to
retain *the tickets*!!

(*Beat.*)

Charles . . . don't look at me l-l-like that!
I didn't lead him on!
He always gives the impression of being l-l-led on
Like a little horse at a circus . . .

(*Beat.*)

I did everything . . .
Then he gave someone a bad cheque
And some very menacing men came round to the flat.
Thugs, my dear
So we left for Tangier
That's the last time I saw him
because there, my dear
Sebastian took up with his new friend
Kurt
A great clod of a German

Ryder

Tangier

TWO

Ryder steps into . . .
  Tangier colours and sounds . . .

Ryder
  I'm looking for Sebastian Flyte
  This is his house . . .?

Kurt
  Yeth.
  But he isn't here

Ryder
  You must be *Kurt*

Kurt
  Yeth

Ryder
  I've come from England on important business
  His mother is very ill.
  Can you tell me where I can find him?

Kurt
  Thebastian's sick
  The holy brothers took him to their infirmary

  (*Sizes up Ryder.*)

  You're not Thebastian's brother?

  (*Panhandling beat.*)

  Cousin?

  (*Ditto.*)

  Maybe you married hith thister?

Ryder
  I'm only a *friend*.
  We were at university together.

Kurt

    I had a friend at university
    A little weak fellow
    I used to pick him up and *shake* him
    Then one day
    We said
    'What the hell
    There is no work in Germany
    Germany is down the drain
    There is no army in Germany now
    We must be *tholdiers*'
    So we joined the Legion
    Then
    My friend died of dysentery
    I said
    What the hell?
    So I shot my foot
    It is now *full* of pus

Ryder

    Yes
    That's very interesting
    But my immediate concern is with Sebastian
    His family sent me
    His mother is very ill

Kurt

    Why don't she give him more money
    Then we could live in *Casablanca* in a nice *flat*

Ryder

    What's wrong with him?

Kurt

    I reckon he drink too much . . .

    (*Ryder moves to . . .*
      A monastery hospital.
      Monks attending.

Sebastian sick in bed.
Ryder looks at him until his eyes open . . .)

Sebastian
I thought when he said 'friend' he meant *Kurt*.
What are *you* doing here, Charles?

Ryder
I came to see *you*

Sebastian
I was out of my mind for a day or two
I kept thinking I was back in Oxford

Ryder
You're very thin

Sebastian
I rather hate *eating*.

Ryder
Otherwise just the same

Sebastian
You're rather more serious
Did you like my house?

Ryder
Very interesting

Sebastian
You look frightfully grown-up

Ryder
You don't

Sebastian
Is Kurt still in my house?

Ryder
The German? Yes.

Sebastian
No one likes Kurt

But
I couldn't get on without him, you know . . .

(*Kurt arrives.*)

Kurt
It is time you came back.
I need you

Sebastian
Do you, Kurt?

Kurt
I reckon so.

Sebastian
What do you want?

Kurt
Cigarettes

Sebastian
I've got some in my bag

(*And tries to reach for them.*)

Ryder
I'll get them.
Where?

Sebastian
No, that's my job

Kurt
Yeth.
I reckon that's *Sebastian's* job.

(*Kurt disappears.*)

Sebastian
If you want something to *do*, Charles,
Straighten out my money

Only – make them sign it to *me personally* . . .
Otherwise
Kurt will get me to sign a cheque for *the whole lot*
When I'm tight
And then he'll go off and get into all kinds of trouble

Ryder
Sebastian . . .
I have some bad news
Your mother is dying . . .

Sebastian
Mummy?
Dying?
I thought she was *an immortal* . . .

Ryder
No.

(*Beat.*)

I said I'd come and try to get you back to England
bef / ore . . .

Sebastian
Still running errands for Mummy, Charles?

Ryder
No.
For *you*.

Sebastian
I don't think I should come back.
I think Mummy is a *femme fatale*!
She kills at *a touch*.
She might try to touch *me*
and I'm really not well, am I?

Ryder
You are supposed *not* to be drinking . . .

Sebastian
> The brothers think I am happier today
> Here's why . . .

> (*Reveals he has a bottle of cognac in bed with him.*)

> Those sweet Arab boys get it for me.

Ryder
> Then – overnight – the telegram . . .
> Sebastian
> I'm most awfully sorry . . .
> Your mother died yesterday evening.

Sebastian (*smiles*)

> Poor Mummy.
> But
> She's now where every Catholic wants to be . . .
> She'll be so pleased

Ryder (*beat*)
> Will you let me take you back to England?

Sebastian
> It would be lovely
> But do you think Kurt would like it?

> (*Ryder quits the space.*
>   *Sebastian disappears.*
>   *Ryder is now in . . .*)

THREE

London.

> *Bridey is there.*

Bridey
> He's not insane?

Ryder
> No

Bridey
  Just weakening himself with drink?

  (*Ryder nods.*)

  And he's found a companion he happens to like?

  (*Ryder nods.*)

  And a place he likes living?

  (*Ryder nods.*
    Bridey thinks and decides . . .)

  Then
  He must have his allowance as you suggest.

  (*Ryder nods.*)

  The thing is quite clear

  (*Ryder nods. Beat.*)

  Would you like to paint Marchmain House?

  (*Ryder nods.*)

Ryder
  Yes
  I should like to very much

Bridey
  Four small oils

Ryder
  Four small oils

Bridey
  That's what my father wants done.
   For a *record*
  To keep at Brideshead.

Ryder
  A record . . .?

Bridey

It's being pulled down.
Marchmain House.
Now Mother's . . .
Father's selling it.
Block of flats in its place.

Ryder

What a sad thing.

Bridey

Well, at least we'll always have *Brideshead*.

(*Beat.*)

You think Marchmain House is good architecturally?

Ryder

One of the most beautiful houses I know

Bridey

Can't see it.
I've always thought it rather ugly.
Perhaps your pictures will make me see it differently.

Ryder

It's my first commission.

Bridey

You'll have to work against time.

Ryder

I will.

(*And colours flood . . . Lines . . . ?*
   Eventually . . .
   Cordelia arrives . . . Watches him . . .)

Cordelia! Hello!

Cordelia

I've come to say 'Goodbye' to old Marchmain!
May I stay here and watch?

Ryder
Yes, if you don't talk.

(*Cordelia tries not to until . . .*)

Cordelia
Itmustbelovelytobeabletodothat

Ryder
It is.
It makes things – *clear*

(*More magic colour.*
    Cordelia watches . . .)

Cordelia
Youwouldn'tliketotakemeto*dinner* would you?

Ryder
Yes.
If you don't talk until I finish this . . .

(*Cordelia watches . . . and tries not to talk until . . .*)

Cordelia
Sebastianwon'tcomehomeevennow?

Ryder
No

Cordelia
Well, Ilovehim *morethananyone.*
RexandJulia are going to take over Brideshead andlive *there.*
They've closedthechapel.
The priest came
He emptied the holywaterstoop
And blew out the lampinthesanctuary . . .

Ryder
Did they?

Cordelia

Noneofthismakes *any* sense to you, Charles!!
You *poor agnostic*

Ryder

Still trying to convert me, Cordelia?

Cordelia

Oh no.
When Papa became a Catholic
He said to Mummy
'You have brought back my family to the faith of their ancestors'
Pompous, youknow.
People leave it in different ways
There's *him*gone
And *Sebastian*gone
And *Julia*gone . . .
And *Mummy*
But God won't let them go *for long*.

Ryder

Won't 'He'?

Cordelia

You waitandsee, you pooragnostic!!!

(*Beat.*)

I got on best with Mummy of any of us
ButIdon'tbelieveIeverreally*loved*her.
Not as she wanted or deserved.
It's odd I didn't.
Because I'm *full*ofnaturalaffection!
I sometimes think when people want to
Hate*God*theyhated*Mummy*
She was *saintly*butshewasn't*a saint*
No one could reallyhate*asaint*
They can't really hate *God* either.

98

When they want to hate Him and His saints
They have to find *something*
Like themselves
And pretend it's *God and* hate *that*.

(*Beat.*)

This will be the first time I've everbeentakenoutto
dinneraloneinarestaurant!!

(*Beat.*)

I hope I've got a vocation
It means I can be a nun

Ryder

You'll fall in love.

Cordelia

Oh pray not!
I say
Do you think I could finish *dinner* with a *scrumptious*
meringue?

FOUR

Cordelia disappears.
  Blanche is revealed.
  A smart crowd . . .

Blanche

So
Charles . . .
You've *enchanted* Society

Ryder

I've merely painted practically
All England's most *beautiful* houses
in all their beautiful grounds . . .

I *love* these buildings that grow silently with the
centuries . . .
Catching and keeping the best of each generation . . .

Blanche

These buildings in, I suspect . . . the last decade of their
grandeur . . .
Trying to *possess* them, Charles?

Ryder

We possess nothing certainly . . . except *the past*
and *memories*

Blanche

Ah memories . . .
Like the pigeons of St Mark's . . .
Everywhere
Under one's feet
Strutting
Perching
If one stands still
On one's sh-sh-sh-shoulder
You've married the fragrant Celia!

(*Celia lights cigarette somewhere . . . in the smart
crowd . . .*)

Celia

Your father's given us the price of a house as a
wedding present
It's too kind of him?
I intend to turn the barn into a studio for you . . .
So you needn't be disturbed by the children . . .
Or when people have to stay.
I understand the artistic temperament.

Ryder

Yes

Blanche

A *Mulcaster*, which is appropriately *ambitious* of you

Ryder
    Is it?

Blanche
    She's made you into a c-c-celebrated '*society*' artist

Ryder
    Has she?
    I've published three *splendid* portfolios
    'Ryder's Country Seats'
    'Ryder's English Homes'
    'Ryder's Provincial Architecture'
    I think *I* contributed *a little* to my . . .

Blanche
    Do you, Charles?

    (*Beat.*)

    Dear Charles . . . each time . . . each 'splendid'
    portfolio . . .
    I r-r-race to see if you'd progressed . . .

Ryder
    I seldom fail to please.

Blanche
    Yes, Charles . . .

Ryder
    Each sold its thousand copies

Blanche
    Yes, Charles

Ryder
    At five guineas apiece

Blanche
    Yes, Charles . . .

Ryder
    I know I've prospered far beyond my merits . . .

Blanche

Well . . .
Your technical skill has grown . . .
And you are *so* enthusiastic about your subject!
But dear Charles . . . *have* you progressed . . . ?

(*Blanche watches Ryder consider this . . .*)

Ryder

I begin to *wonder* . . .
I begin to mourn my 'art' . . .
Its fading light . . .

Blanche

Ah . . . Art!

Ryder

I'm in no great pains to stay in touch with England.

(*Ryder and Blanche look towards Celia, who waves to them. They both wave back as . . .*)

Blanche

There are wh-wh-whispers about your wife . . .

Ryder

Are there?
I think she thinks nobody notices . . .

Blanche

Dear Celia
Doesn't she *know* it's a *m-m-minuscule* world . . . ?

(*And the smart crowd dissolve.*)

FIVE

Ryder alone . . .

Ryder

I've no settled route
I drift like a cast-off boat

On a dark sea
Pushed by *this* tide, dragged by *that* . . .
I end up in South America . . .
I paint
And paint
And paint and
After two years
I meet up with my wife again
And see the fruits of our separation in New York . . .

SIX

Celia looking at paintings.

    Ryder watching Celia looking at paintings . . .

Celia

I can see they're perfectly *brilliant* . . .
Really rather *beautiful* . . . in a sinister way
But . . . I don't feel they are quite *you*.

Ryder

Really?

Celia

I don't believe you read my letters.

Ryder

Some went astray . . .
I remember
The daffodils in the orchard were *a dream*.
The nursery maid was *a jewel*.
Your new baby is called . . .

Celia

Caroline . . .

Ryder

Why *Caroline?*

(*Beat.*)

Celia

After *Charles* of course

Ryder

Ah

Very clever

Celia

I made Bertha Van Halt godmother.

I thought she was safe for a good present.

What do you think she gave?

Ryder

Bertha Van Halt is a well known *trap*.

What?

Celia

A fifteen-shilling book token! Now that Johnjohn has a companion . . .

Ryder

Who?

Celia

Your *son*, darling.

You haven't forgotten him too?

Ryder

For Christ's sake, why do you call him that?

Celia

It's a name he invented for himself.

He talks of you a lot.

He prays every night for your safe return.

(*Beat.*)

Shall I put my face to bed?

Ryder

No. Not at once.

(*Celia efficiently prepares to service her husband.*)

She knows what is wanted.
She has neat, hygienic ways for that too.
Afterwards
We lay on our twin beds
A yard or two distant . . .

Celia

Were you at all frightened at meeting me today?

Ryder

Not the least.

Celia

You didn't wonder if I should have fallen in love with
someone else in the meantime?

Ryder

No. Have you?

Celia

You know I haven't. Have you?

Ryder

No. I'm not in love.
Then we board our ship to sail for England . . .

SEVEN

A ship departing . . .
  Noises . . .
  Crowd waving.
    Into . . .

Celia

Such a lot of friends!
It's going to be a *lovely* trip!
Let's have a cocktail party this evening . . .

(*Telephone* . . .)

Julia,
This is Celia . . . Celia Ryder
It's *lovely* to find you on board.
What have you been up to?

(*Listens until* . . .)

Come and have a cocktail this evening and tell me all
about it.

Ryder
Julia who?

Celia
Mottram
I haven't seen her for years.

Cocktail Guests Various:
Our stateroom is *enor* / *mous* / the bath is rather /
small / yes, we *are* at the captain's table / isn't the ice
swan too / amusing? / playing baccarat after this?
They say its going to be as smooth as a millpond all
the way!!

(*And Julia appears* . . .)

Julia
Charles
I never see you now
I never seem to see anyone I like

Ryder
What have you been doing in America?

Julia
Don't you *know*?
I've been *a mug*.
I thought I was in love with someone other than *Rex*
But it didn't turn out that way
I long to see the paintings
Celia is as pretty as ever

She hasn't changed
You have
So lean and *grim*
Harder

Ryder

And you're softer?

Julia

Yes, I think so.
And very *patient* now . . .

Ryder

She seems to say

Julia

Look at me.
I have done my share.
I am beautiful.
It is something quite out of the ordinary, this beauty
of mine.
I am made for delight.
But what do I get out of it?
Where is my reward?

Ryder

That is the change in her from ten years ago
that, indeed, is her reward
this haunting, magical stillness
which speaks straight to my heart
and strikes silence there . . .
it is the completion of her beauty . . .
Sadder too

Julia

Oh yes, much sadder.

Ryder

And then we two ships

Julia

Collide

Celia

Either I am a little drunk
Or it's getting rough

Ryder

We find ourselves leaning sideways in our chairs
There is a crash and tinkle of falling cutlery
The gale
Unheard /
Unseen
Unfelt
Has been mounting over us . . .

Society Various

Oh what's happening? / I say? I say I don't like this one
little bit! / *Millpond??* / I'm feeling a little bit / What *is*
the captain thinking of?

Ryder

Veers
And falls
Full on our bows

(*Fearful storm . . .*)

Celia

I didn't know a ship of this size could pitch like this
I feel *terrible*
Can't you *do* something?!!

Ryder

I ring for the night steward
All night between dreaming and waking I think of
Julia . . .
Flowers come for my wife
I remove the card from the roses and send them with
my love
To Julia . . .

Celia

Charles, aren't you coming to see me?

Ryder

    I came once.
    I'll be in again.

Celia

    Don't bother.
    Come in sometimes and tell me what's going on.

EIGHT

Ryder and Julia sitting, talking . . .

Julia

    Rex simply isn't *all there*
    He isn't a complete human being *at all*
    He's a tiny *bit* of one
    Unnaturally developed
    Something *in a bottle*
    An *organ* kept alive in a *laboratory*
    I *thought* he was a sort of primitive savage
    But he is something absolutely
    Modern and up-to-date
    That only *this* ghastly age could produce

    (*Ryder kisses her.*)

Julia

    No, Charles, not yet.
    I don't know if I *want* love.

Ryder

    Love?
    I'm not asking for *love.*

Julia

    Oh yes, Charles, you are.

Ryder

    Another climb
    Another vast drop

Celia

I feel terrible
I didn't know a ship this size could pitch like this!
Are you awake?
Can't you do something?
Can't you get something from the doctor?

Julia

Everyone's seasick.

Ryder

Everyone but us
As the storm rages on . . . we are

Julia

talking

Ryder

What had we to say?

Julia

Rex has never been unkind to me *intentionally* . . .
It's just
He isn't a *real* person at all.
Just a few faculties highly developed
The rest isn't *there*.

Ryder

I was *glad* when I found Celia was unfaithful
I felt it was alright to dislike her

Julia

Is she?
Do you?
I'm *glad*.
I don't like her either.
Why did you marry her?

Ryder

Physical attraction.

Ambition.
Everyone agrees she's the perfect wife for a painter.
Loneliness
Missing Sebastian . . .

(*Beat.*)

Julia
You loved him, didn't you?

Ryder
Oh yes.
He was the forerunner to *this*.

Celia
Charles, are you there?

Ryder
Yes.

Celia
I've been asleep such a long time.
It's no better, is it?

Ryder
Worse.

Celia
Are you having an amusing evening?

Ryder
Everyone's seasick

Celia
Poor Charles

Julia
We thought Papa might come back to England after
Mummy died
I've grown fond of him
Sebastian's disappeared *completely*
Cordelia's in Spain with *an ambulance*

Bridey leads his own extraordinary life collecting
matchbox covers . . .
Rex and I live at Brideshead now. Rex gives parties . . .
The cigar smoke
Do I smell of it now?

Ryder

You smell wonderful

(*Beat.*)

Julia

I was faithful to him until this last thing came along . . .
which is more than I can say for *him* . . .

(*Beat.*)

There's *nothing like a good upbringing*

(*Beat.*)

Last year
I decided to have a child . . .
I'd decided to have it brought up a Catholic
I thought
'That's *one* thing I can give her.
It doesn't seem to have done me much good but my
child shall have it . . .'
odd – giving something one had lost oneself.

(*Beat.*)

In the end
I couldn't even give her that
Couldn't even give her life . . .

(*Beat.*
    Ryder takes her hand.)

I've been punished a little for marrying Rex you see . . .

(*Beat.*)

Now I suppose I shall be punished for what I've just
done.

(*Beat.*)

Perhaps that's why you and I are here like this
Part of a plan
Perhaps God sent this storm . . .
Look . . .
Sunset.

(*Fabulous sunset . . .*)

Ryder
The end of our day.

(*Beat.*)

Now?

Julia
Yes, *now.*

Ryder
There is a formality to be observed, no more.
It is as though a deed of conveyance
Of her narrow loins
Had been drawn and sealed.
I am making my first entry as a freeholder of a property
I will enjoy and develop at leisure.
The stars come out
And sweep across the sky as once
I remember
I had seen them sweep above the towers and gables
of Oxford

Sebastian

Brideshead

The ship is sailing smoothly now.

Celia
Charles, Charles
I feel so well

What do you think I am having for breakfast?
A beefsteak!!

Julia

Oh dear
Where can we hide in fair weather
We orphans of the storm?

NINE

Another private view.

Ryder arrives to . . .

Celia

We are out to catch critics this time
Its *high time* they took you seriously and they *know* it

(*Beat.*)

Whose car was that you came in?

Ryder

Julia's

Celia

Julia's?

(*Beat.*)

Why didn't you bring her in?
I've just been listening to a Mr Samgrass
wax lyrical about the 'Brideshead Set'.
What *would* Teresa Marchmain have thought?

Ryder

I'm going there tonight

Celia

To *Brideshead*?

Ryder

Yes

Celia

Not *tonight*?!

Ryder

Yes, tonight.
It's all settled.

(*A photographer brings them together.*
They stand together smiling as . . .
Flash of a lamp in their faces.
They stand apart as . . .)

Art Crowd Various

Splendid / Very strong / Most exotic /
If you'd asked me to guess . . .
Ryder's / Charles Ryder? / The Charles Ryder? Yes!
Is the last name would have / occurred to me . . .
They're so vir / ile
So passion / ate . . .
Such *Art*!

Celia

Darling I *must* go.
It's been a *terrific* success, hasn't it?

Ryder

Terrific

Celia

I'll think of something to tell them at home.

Ryder

Good

Celia

I wish it hadn't got to happen *quite* this way . . .

(*And she vanishes.*)

Ryder

She knows
She's had her nose down since luncheon
She's picked up the scent.

(Blanche breaks through the throng . . .)

Blanche

No, I have *not* brought a card of invitation.
I do *not* want my photograph in the *Tatler*
I have *not* come to exhibit myself
I have come to see the *pictures*
Charles!!
At *l-l-lunch*
All the talk was of *you*
'*Poor* Celia after all she's done for him'
'And with *Julia* after the way she behaved in *America*.'
I hear that you have gone to the Tropics
And returned *a Gauguin*??
Let me see!!

(And he stands in front of each one of the works.
   And . . . looks and looks and looks until . . .
   Ryder watches him looking . . .)

Where, my dear Charles
Did you find this sumptuous greenery?
The corner of a hothouse in *Tring*?

Ryder

South America

(Blanche sighs deeply.
   And again.
   And again.)

Blanche

But they tell me, my d-d-dear, you are happy *in love*
That is *everything*, is it not?

Ryder

Are they as bad as that?

Blanche

My dear, let us not expose your little imposture
Before these good plain people

We know, you and I.
This is the most terrible t-t-t-tripe
I went to your first exhibition, you know,
Four interiors of Marchmain House
Very *English* very *correct*
But *charming*
'Charles has done something,' I said,
'Not all he *will* do, not all he *can* do, but *something* . . .
What will he do next?'

(*Sighs again.*)

Your exhibition reminds me of dear Sebastian when he
liked so much to dress up in false whiskers!
Or get his teddy bear to have opinions
It's *charm*
Simple creamy English *charm* playing tigers

Ryder
You're quite right.

Blanche
My dear . . . Of *course* I'm right
I warned you of charm all those years ago
I warned you *expressly* and in great detail of the Flyte
family.
Charm is the great English blight.
It spots and kills *anything* it touches.
It kills *love*
It kills *art*
I greatly fear, dear Charles, it has killed you.

TEN

Ryder joins Julia at Brideshead.

Brideshead Set Various (*making an enormous racket*)
We had our chance in Oc / tober. Why didn't we send
the Italian fleet to the bottom of the / Mare Nostrum?

Boom! / Ha / ha!
Franco's simply a German / agent!
The people are with / him!
The press are with / him!
I'm with / him!
Who cares about divorce now except a few old maids /
who aren't married anyway?

(*As . . .*)

Ryder
Darling
Celia knows
Everyone seems to know

Julia
Damn everybody

Ryder
What about Rex?

(*Rex emerges through the throng.*)

Hello, Rex.

Rex
It's great to have you back, Charles. Like the old days!
Bridey's due at the weekend . . . for the Agricultural . . .
Will you still be here?
I expect so from what I gather.

(*Beat.*)

Well, meet the throng . . .
Tonight we have some politicians for you . . .

(*Waves and gets back appropriate waves as . . .*)

Bags of 'young' Conservatives . . .
a Socialist! from the coal mines
just the *one* financier . . . but he's stinking rich . . .
oh and a society columnist . . . love-sick for the
Socialist . . .

one lone woman . . . if anyone's interested in that sort /
of hunting!!
Julia, show Charles round.

Ryder
I wonder which is the more horrible . . .
Celia's Art and Fashion
Or Rex's Politics and Money?

Rex / Brideshead Set
All we want is a showdown
We had our chance in October!
Why didn't we blow Spezia to blazes??
Franco's simply a German agent.
That bluff's been called!
It would make the monarchy stronger!
The Press are with him!
I'm with him!
Who cares about divorce now??
Why didn't we close the Canal??
Why didn't we bomb Rome!
We need a showdown!
With Baldwin . . .
With Hitler
With the Old Gang . . .

Ryder
Why is it that love makes me hate the whole world?

Julia
I feel the past and the future pressing so hard on either
side
There's no room for the present at all!

Ryder
We've got our happiness in spite of them
They can't hurt us, can they?

ELEVEN

More intimate Brideshead.
   Bridey, Julia, Ryder . . .

Bridey
   Julia, where are Mummy's jewels?

Julia
   This was hers.

   (*Her bracelet.*)

   And this.

   (*Her necklace.*)

   Cordelia and I had all her own things.
   The family jewels went to the bank.

Bridey
   Aren't there some rather famous jewels?

Julia
   Yes.
   A necklace.

Bridey
   I'd like to have a look at them

Julia
   Bridey, why?
   Don't be so mysterious!

Bridey
   I'm engaged to be married . . .

Julia
   How . . . how very exciting!

Ryder
   Well done, Bridey!

Julia

Who to?

Bridey

Nobody you know . . .

Julia

Is she pretty?

Bridey

I don't think you would exactly call her pretty.
'Comely' is the word I think of in her connexion.
She is a big woman.

Julia

Fat?

Bridey

No, big.
She is called Mrs Muspratt.
Her Christian name is Beryl.
Widow.

Julia

But, Bridey, where did you find her?

Bridey

Her late husband Admiral Muspratt, collected
matchboxes

Julia

You're not marrying her for her matchboxes . . .?

(*Julia and Ryder stifle laughter, even during . . .*)

Bridey

No no, the whole collection was left to Falmouth
Town Library.
I have great affection for her.
She is very cheerful
Very fond of acting

She is connected with the Catholic Players Guild.
She has three sons!
Eldest just gone to Ampleforth.

Julia

Does Papa know?

Bridey

I wrote.
He has written back.
I have his approval.
He has been urging me to marry for some time.
She's just about my own age.

(*With great forbearance, they don't laugh.*)

Julia

Bridey, you sly smug old brute . . . Why haven't you
brought her *here*?

Bridey

Oh, I couldn't.

(*Beat.*)

Julia

You couldn't.
Why, Bridey . . . ?

Bridey

It is a matter of indifference to me whether you choose
to live in sin with Rex or Charles or . . .

(*He can't quite say 'both'.*)

But in no case would Beryl consent to be your guest.

Julia

You pompous ass.

(*Julia moves in tears to another space.*)

Ryder

Bridey, what a bloody offensive thing to say to Julia.

Bridey

I am merely stating a fact well-known to her . . .

(*Ryder joins Julia.*)

Ryder

How *dare* he speak to you like that?

Julia

He's quite right.
Bridey and his widow
they've got it in black and white.
they bought it for a penny at the church door.
put a penny in the box
take your tract.

(*Beat.*)

I want to marry you, Charles.

Ryder

One day, darling.

Julia

Now!
Marriage isn't a thing we can 'take' when the impulse
moves us.
There must be a *divorce* . . . two divorces.
We must make plans.
You must talk to Rex.

TWELVE

Ryder joins Rex.

Rex

Why bring Julia and *me* into this?
If Celia wants to marry again, well and good, let her
Julia and I are quite happy *as we are*,
You *can't* say I've been difficult,

I've had my own fish to fry too.
But a *divorce*?
Different thing *altogether*
Charles, old boy, it's a . . .
Difficult time for me . . .
Things *here* get *talked* about there's rather
Too much about *me* in the Press . . .
I need to look *good* for my party chiefs you know?
A *war* would set everything straight for me but . . .
Charles . . . I've
Never known a divorce here in this country to do
anyone any good . . .

Ryder

Julia's set on it.

Rex

What I hope is . . .
You might be able to talk her round . . .?
Tell her to hang on a bit, Charles.
There's a good fellow . . .
I can't look up from the table . . .
I'll just melt away, shall I?

THIRTEEN

Ryder with a newly arrived Cordelia.
  Bridge over a river.

Cordelia

This is *lovely* but I'm missing my ambulance *terribly.*

Ryder

So nice to have you back, Cordelia . . .

Cordelia

I've visited Sebastian . . .
Do *you* want to know about him?

Ryder

No.

(*Beat.*)

Yes.

Cordelia

He's in Tunis
With the monks
He's got a beard and he's very religious . . .
They love him
He's still loved wherever he goes
Whatever condition he's in . . .
People like him
They're very near and dear to God . . .
There's nothing anyone can do for him now
But *pray* . . .

Ryder

Pray

Cordelia

Yes

Ryder

I suppose he doesn't suffer

Cordelia

Oh yes, I think he does
No one is ever holy without suffering

(*She sees Ryder needs some comfort.*)

He's in a very beautiful place
By the sea
White cloisters
A bell tower
Rows of green vegetables
And a monk watering them when the sun is low

Ryder

He's with me daily.

Cordelia

In . . . Julia

Ryder

I haven't forgotten him

(*Beat.*)

Cordelia

I once had a governess who jumped off this bridge and
drowned herself

Ryder

I know
It was the first thing I knew about you

Cordelia

Are you thinking
'Poor Cordelia . . .?
Plain pious spinster?
so
thwarted' . . .?

(*Beat.*)

Ryder

Yes

(*Beat.*)

Cordelia

That's exactly the word I think of for you and Julia.
Thwarted

(*Beat.*)

Charles . . .
Surely God made us for some other purpose than this?

(*Beat.*)

I've come back to Brideshead *for a reason*, Charles.
Papa is worried about the international situation.
And he's rather ill.
He's coming back to Brideshead.

FOURTEEN

Lord Marchmain, wrapped up but shivering, tears in his eyes.
  Cara ditto but tearless.
  He raises his gloved hand in a tiny acknowledgment.

Lord Marchmain
  It's the cold.
  I'd forgotten how cold it is in England!
  Clara, where are those confounded pills?

(*He sits down in an unused ornamental chair.*)

Cara
  He has come home to die

Ryder
  What is it?

Cara
  His heart. Some long word of the heart.
  He is dying of a long word.

Lord Marchmain
  Plender, get a bed made for me downstairs.

Plender
  Very good, My Lord.
  Which room shall we put it in?

Lord Marchmain (*ponders for a bit*)
  The Chinese Drawing Room.
  And

Wilcox . . .
The Queen's Bed

Wilcox
The Chinese Drawing Room?
My Lord, the Queen's Bed?

Lord Marchmain
Yes, yes.
I may be spending some time there in the next few weeks.
Cordelia, will you watch for an hour?

(*And the Queen's Bed is assembled before our eyes . . .*)

FIFTEEN

Cordelia
He fell asleep at once.
I came in at two to make up the fire
The lights were on.

(*Beat.*)

I think perhaps he is afraid of the dark . . .

(*And they join Lord Marchmain, who is in the Queen's Bed . . .*)

Lord Marchmain
Brideshead and his wife dined with me in Rome.
Since we are all members of the family . . .

(*His eyes dwell for a moment on Ryder, and Cara.*)

I can speak without reserve.
I found her deplorable.
I suppose I must call her . . . Beryl . . .

Cordelia
Yes, Papa, you must.

Lord Marchmain
I daresay I shall not be really fit
Again until summer comes . . .
In Italy no one believes there will be a war . . .
I look to you four to amuse me . . .
I suppose you no longer have access to political
information, Julia?
Cara, here is fortunately a British subject by marriage.
Mrs Hicks

Cara
I don't customarily mention this . . .

Lord Marchmain
It may prove valuable . . .
And *you*
You will no doubt become an official war artist?

Ryder
No.
As a matter of fact
I am now negotiating for a commission in the Special
Reserve.

Lord Marchmain
Ah, but you *should* be an artist.
I had one with my squadron in the last war
Until we went up to the line!
Matchboxes *matchboxes*
I think she's past childbearing . . .
Who shall I leave this place to?
Sebastian alas is out of the question.
Would *you* like it, Cara?
Cordelia?
I think I shall leave it to Julia and Charles.

Julia
Papa . . . it's *Bridey's*.

Lord Marchmain
I have rather a fancy for installing *Julia* here . . .

Ryder
Does he mean it?

Julia
Yes, I think he does.
But it's *monstrous* for Bridey . . .

Ryder
Is it?

Julia
It's Papa's to leave it as he likes.

Ryder
I think you and I could be very happy here.
I love Brideshead.
I love you.

SIXTEEN

Ryder
Lord Marchmain continues changing his mind
And . . . continues . . . dying . . .

Julia
I think Papa likes us all to be in the room with him

Ryder
Lord Marchmain did not wish us to speak.
But he talked.

Lord Marchmain
Better today.
We live long and marry late.
Seventy-three is no great age!

Ryder
>He talks I think
>Because his is the only voice he can trust . . .

Lord Marchmain
>. . . Aunt *Julia* lived to be eighty-eight!
>Never married
>Born and died here!
>Saw the *fire* on beacon hill for the Battle of *Trafalgar*.
>
>Always called *this* house 'The New House'
>It was a century old when she was born . . .
>'The New House'!!
>
>The old house was near the church . . .
>*cross-legged* knight
>*doubleted* earl . . .
>marquis like a Roman senator in *Italian marble* . . .
>we were knights then . . . *barons* since *Agincourt*!!
>The *fountain* came from Naples on a man-of-war!
>
>Better today
>I shall live long
>Always ate moderately
>Fine claret
>Slept in my own sheets . . .
>
>I was *fifty* when they dismounted us and sent us up the line . . .
>The orders
>'Old men stay at the base'
>but my commanding officer said . . .
>'You're as fit as the youngest of 'em, Alex'
>so I was
>so I am
>If I could only breathe
>
>Plender
>Open the windows

Plender
The windows are open, My Lord.

SEVENTEEN

Bridey
He's fading

(*Stands looking at Lord Marchmain.*)

He must see a priest.

Cordelia
Not yet.
Papa doesn't want him yet.

Ryder
Can't they even let him die in peace?

Julia
They mean something so different by 'peace'.

Ryder
They'll come and claim him
When his strength can't resist
To claim him as 'a deathbed penitent'!
Its all superstition and trickery!!
. . . Don't you a / gree?

Julia
I don't *know*, Charles, I simply *don't know*.

Bridey
I'll take Father Mackay to him tomorrow.

Ryder
Julia
How can we stop this *tomfoolery*?

Julia
Why should we?

Ryder

It's such witchcraft and / hypocrisy!

Julia

Is it?

Its been going on for *two thousand years*

Why are you in such a rage now??

Write a letter to *The Times*!!

Make a speech in Hyde Park!!

But don't bore *me* about it!!

Ryder

Julia, what's wrong?

Julia

Daddy is dying *in sin*!

Mummy died with *my sin* eating at her!

Christ died with it

Nailed *hand and foot*!!

We're living in *sin*

I *hate* it.

(*She hits him, suddenly, violently, across the face.
Beat.*)

Now do you see how I hate it?

(*Beat.*)

Your poor face.

(*Beat.*)

Will there be a mark tomorrow?

EIGHTEEN

Lord Marchmain's bed.

People circling it.

Cordelia brings in Father Mackay.

Cordelia
Papa . . . I have brought Father Mackay to see you.

Lord Marchmain
Father Mackay
I am afraid you have been brought here under
a misapprehension
I am *not* in extremis
And have *not* been a practising member of your
Church for twenty-five years

(*Father Mackay vanishes* . . .)

Julia
Do you remember the storm?

Ryder
Yes.

Julia
Do you remember
In our first year together
You hung about Naples?

Ryder
Yes . . .
and we met

Julia / Ryder
'by arrangement'

Ryder
on the hill path

Julia
I went back to the villa, said,
'Papa, who do you think has arrived at the hotel?'
And he said

Lord Marchmain
'Charles Ryder, I suppose'

Julia
I said
'Why did you think of him?'
and Papa replied

Lord Marchmain
Cara came back from Paris with the news you were
inseparable
He seems to have a penchant for my children
However, bring him here.

Ryder
Julia . . .

Julia
Do you remember how the sun came out
On our last evening
. . . just as it has done today?

NINETEEN

*Cordelia, Cara, Julia, Ryder in a very cross, tense family
row . . .*

Ryder (*triumphant*)
Hurrah!
Mumbo-jumbo is *off*
The *witch doctor* has gone

Bridey
What Papa *said* was
'I am not in extremis
And have not been a practising member of *the* Church /
for twenty-five years'

Ryder
Not '*the* Church', '*your* Church'

Bridey

I don't see the differ / ence

Julia

There's *every* difference

Ryder

Bridey, it's quite plain what he meant.

Bridey

He meant what he *said*
He had not been accustomed to regularly to receive the sacraments
And since he was not at the moment of dying
He did not mean to change his / ways yet

Ryder

That's simply *a quibble*

Bridey

It's *precise*
He did not want to see a priest that day
But he would when he is in ext / remis

Ryder

So if he dies alone he goes to hell
If the priest puts the oil / on him

Cordelia

Oh, it's not the oil
That's to heal / him

Cara

If the priest gets there before the body is cold it is all right.
That's so, isn't it?

Cordelia

No, Cara, it's *not*

Julia

Of *course* / not.

Bridey
You've got it all wrong, / Cara.

Cara
When Alphonse de Grenet died
Madame de G had a priest hidden outside the door
Alphonse couldn't *bear* the sight of a priest
And they brought him in before the body was cold
They had a full Requiem for him
I went to it

Cordelia
Having a Requiem doesn't mean you go to hea / ven

Cara
Madame de Grenet thought it did

Julia
Well she was *wrong.*

Ryder
Do any of you *Catholics* know what *good* you think
this priest can do??
Bridey??

Bridey tells me at some length

TWENTY

*The watchers at the bedside rearrange into another
formation.*
Everyone even more frazzled . . .

Cara (*slight wonder*)
I never heard that before!

Ryder
Let's get this *clear*
He has to make *an act of will*

He has to be *contrite* and *wish* to be reconciled
Is that right?

(*Various degrees of certainty / doubt mumbled . . .*)

But only God knows whether he has really made an
act of will
The priest can't tell.

(*Again the mumbled certainty / doubt.*)

And if there isn't a priest there
And he makes an act of will alone
That's as good as if there was a priest
And it's quite possible that the will may still be
working when a man
Is too weak to make an outward sign of it
Is that right?

(*Again.*)

He may be lying
As though dead
And willing all the time
And being reconciled
And God understands that . . .
Is that right?

(*Beat.*)

Bridey
More or less

Ryder
Well, for heaven's sake . . .
What is the priest for?

(*Pause.
    Julia sighs.
    Bridey takes a breath.*)

Cara
   All I know is that I shall take very good care
   To have a priest.

TWENTY-ONE

And another rearrangement around the bed.
   Julia and Ryder alone.

Julia
   I wish you wouldn't start these religious arguments

Ryder
   I only want to *know* what these people *believe!!*

Julia
   If you'd let Bridey / *finish* –

Ryder
   There were *four* of you!
   Cara didn't know *the first thing*
   You knew a bit and didn't believe *a word*
   Cordelia just believed *madly*
   And Bridey knew and believed and explained it
   dreadfully
   People go round saying
   'At least Catholics know what they believe!'

Julia
   Oh Charles, don't rant!
   I shall begin to believe you're getting doubts yourself.

TWENTY-TWO

And another , . .
   Julia with her father.
   Rex and Ryder on the periphery.

Ryder

Meanwhile . . .

A game of 'General Post . . .'

Moving my property from the Old Rectory to my flat

My wife's from my flat to the Old Rectory

Julia's from Rex's house and Brideshead to my flat . . .

Rex's from Brideshead to his house . . .

Mrs Muspratt's from Falmouth to Brideshead . . .

As

My divorce and Julia's became absolute

TWENTY-THREE

Another group. Ryder and Cordelia.

Ryder

He's got a wonderful will to *live*, hasn't he?

Cordelia

I should say a great fear of *death*.

Ryder

Is there a difference?

Cordelia

Ohdearyes.

He doesn't derive any strength fromhisfear,youknow.

It's wearing him out.

Lord Marchmain

Cordelia, what became of the chapel?

Cordelia

They locked it up, Papa. When Mummy died.

Lord Marchmain

I built it for *her.*

Then I went away

Left her in the chapel *praying.*

I never came back to disturb her prayers.
Was it a crime?

Cordelia
I think it was, Papa.

Lord Marchmain
Is that why they've locked me in this cave, do you
think?

TWENTY-FOUR

And another . . .

Doctor
I think this may be it . . .

Julia
I'm sending for Father Mackay!

Ryder
Doctor
I think it will kill him
We must stop this nonsense.

Doctor
Then will *you* forbid it?

Ryder
I have *no authority*
Cara, what do you think?

Cara
I don't want him made unhappy.

(*Beat.*)

I should like a priest here all the same

Ryder
I've telegraphed for Bridey and Cordelia

Nothing must be done until they are here

(*Beat.*)

The shock of seeing a priest may kill / him.

Julia
Cara?

Cara
Alex was not a religious man.
He scoffed *always*.
If Father Mackay could come to him / unconscious . . .?

(*Julia arrives with Father Mackay.*)

Father Mackay
Now
How could I be a shock to anyone?
I want to do something so small
I just want to ask him if he is sorry for his sins
I want him to make some little sign of assent
Then I want to give him God's pardon
Then
I want to *anoint* him
It is *nothing*
A touch of the fingers
Just some oil from this little box
Look
It is nothing to hurt / him

Cara
Oh Julia
What are we to say?

Julia
I take full responsibility for whatever happens.
Father Mackay
Will you please come and see my father now?

Ryder
  Without looking at me
  She led him to the bed.

  (*Lord Marchmain, very still . . .*
      All but Ryder kneeling . . .)

  There's a wall of fire between Julia and me.

Father Mackay
  Now
  I know you are sorry for all the sins of your life
  Aren't you?
  Make a sign if you can . . .
  You're sorry, aren't you?

Ryder
  There's no sign

Father Mackay
  I am going to give you absolution.
  While I am giving it
  Tell God you are sorry you have offended him
  Ego te absolvo in nomine Patris.

  (*He makes the sign of the cross.*)

Ryder (*kneels too, prays . . .*)
  O God
  If there is a god
  Forgive him his sins
  If there is such a thing as sin.

  And the man on the bed opens his eyes
  And gives a sigh

  (*Marchmain sighs.*)

  The sort of sigh I had imagined men make at the hour
  of their death
  But his eyes move

143

(*Marchmain's eyes move.*)

I suddenly feel a longing for a sign
It seems so small a thing to ask

(*Prays.*)

God forgive him his sins
Please God make him accept Your forgiveness . . .

The priest touches the dying man with an oily wad
Gives the final blessing
suddenly
Lord Marchmain . . .

(*Lord Marchmain's hand moves slowly down his breast.
    Then to his shoulder
    And he makes the sign of the cross . . .*)

And then I know
That the sign I had asked for is *not* a little thing.

(*Lord Marchmain dies.*)

TWENTY-FIVE

Ryder and Julia face one another . . .

Julia
A minute to say goodbye

Ryder
So long to say so little

Julia
You knew?

Ryder
Since this morning . . .

(*Beat.*)

No.
All year.

Julia

I didn't know until today.
I can't marry you, Charles.
I can't be with you ever again

Ryder

I know

Julia

I *can't* live in *sin* . . .
not just *doing wrong* like I did in America . . .
but *knowing* it . . .
'Poor Julia' they're saying
'She can't go out
She's got to take care of *her sin*.
A pity it ever *lived*,' they say
'But, it's so *strong*.
Children like that always are.
Julia's so good to her little mad sin.'
I *can't* shut myself out from His mercy.
I can't have a life with *you*
without *Him*.
I believe . . .
If I give up this *one* thing I want *so much* . . .
He won't *quite* despair of me in the end

Ryder

Now we shall both be alone

Julia

I have no way of making you understand

Ryder

I don't want to make it easier for you
I hope your heart may break
But I do understand.

TWENTY-SIX

Ryder is back in the same place as in in the first scene.

Ryder
 Brideshead
 They made a new house with the stones of the old one.
 The builders . . .
 Perhaps that's the pleasure of *building*
 Like having *a son*
 Wondering how he'll grow up . . .
 I don't *know*,
 I've forfeited the right to watch my son grow up
 I'm homeless
 Childless
 Middle-aged
 Loveless
 I've never built anything
 No house
 No chapel.

 (*The chapel.*
  Ryder regards the red flame burning there . . .
  He genuflects.
  He prays.
  Lights fade.)

End of play.